Brilliant! Encouraging you toward unique and creative thinking, so that ONE DAY… *Bold!* Challenging you to break the boundaries, so that ONE DAY… *Blessed!* The God-inspired vision of a leader who's ONE DAY has come.
May it spread up over.

> *– Commissioner Joe Noland*
> *JoeNoland.com*

From a passion guided and empowered by the Holy Spirit, Commissioner James Knaggs has crafted a personal and corporate dream – a dream that was promptly embraced by the soldiers of the Australian Southern Territory. While the dream is a powerful, far-reaching Vision Statement for the Australian Southern Territory, it should be embraced as a vision for every territory and command around the Army world. It is a pleasure to enthusiastically endorse this kingdom and Army building vision statement. My prayer is that each aspect of the dream becomes a reality throughout the Australian Southern Territory, and indeed in The Salvation Army throughout the world.

> *– Commissioner William W. Francis*
> *Territorial Commander, Canada and Bermuda*

I hear the rumbling from 'down under'. A revived, Holy Spirit filled Salvation Army of believers is rising with a fresh vision and passion for not only what can be - but what ought to be! It always happens when God gives a dream. For the sake of the Kingdom to Come ... don't let these dreams die!

- Commissioner Israel L. Gaither
National Commander, United States of America

The vision set out in this short publication vibrates with spiritual life and holy ambition. May it become a reality more and more as the days go by and as Salvationists in every part of the world continue to seek the will of God.

Let the prayers of all Salvationists uphold those working to achieve every aspect of the vision. I firmly believe that one day it will come true, and this sooner than we might expect if God is given his way among us. Work on, pray on, keeping your faith high in the power of the Lord.

- Shaw Clifton
General

As a former Territorial Commander of the Australia Southern Territory (and Training Principal of Commissioners James and Carolyn Knaggs), it is a privilege to add my endorsement to the concepts contained in the dream of Commissioner James Knaggs.

We of course have a part to play if this dream is to be realised. "If my people which are called by my name shall HUMBLE THEMSELVES and PRAY and SEEK MY FACE and TURN FROM THEIR WICKED WAYS; then will I hear from heaven and will forgive their sin and will heal their land." (2 Chron.7:14)

As you meditate on the vision that God has given to Commissioner Knaggs, may there be a whole-hearted, positive response of heart and mind to the challenge presented.

The concepts contained in this dream certainly have Biblical backing. They reveal something of the heart of God for the Southern Territory.

My prayer is that there may be a mighty moving of the Spirit in your midst during these challenging days.

- Bramwell H. Tillsley
General (Rtd)

Commissioner Knaggs has cast a thorough, thoughtful and exciting vision for the future of the Army to which the Salvationists of Australia must now respond, not only in words, but in creative, costly and Christ-honouring action.

- Paul A. Rader
General (Rtd)

As a fellow missioner, I am excited to read the Dream of my friend, Commissioner Jim Knaggs. My spirit is lifted and challenged to prayer and action for the cause of Christ and the mission of The Salvation Army in the pursuit of the day when this dream will be a reality.

God bless the Australia Southern Territory.

- Commissioner Lawrence R. Moretz
USA Eastern Territory

A dream worth living for the Australia Southern Territory

One Day...

Olivia & Dick

God's Blessings!

Jim

Commissioner Jim Knaggs
& 35 Salvationists of the Australia Southern Territory.

2007: SALVO Publishing.

Copyright © 2007 - The Salvation Army Australia Southern Territory.

All rights reserved. Except for fair dealing permitted under the Copyright Act, no part of this book may be reproduced by any means without permission in writing from author/publisher.

First published 2007
Second Edition published 2008

National Library of Australia
Cataloguing-in-Publication date

Knaggs, James, 1950- .

ONE DAY... : A dream worth living for the Australia Southern Territory

ISBN 978-0-9585991-5-3
1. Holiness - Christianity. I. The Salvation Army. Australia Southern Territory. II. Title.

For Worldwide Distribution

This book and other Salvation Army resources are available from salvationarmy.org.au

Scripture quotations marked (NLT) are taken from the Holy Bible, New Living Translation, copyright 1996. Used by permission of Tyndale House Publishers, Inc., Wheaton, Illinois 60189. All rights reserved.

Subediting: The Salvation Army National Editorial Department, Australia

Set in Baka Too and Adobe Caslon Pro.

Design and layout by Simon Robertson of the Australia Southern Territory Corps Programme Department

The Salvation Army
Australia Southern Territory
SALVO Publishing

salvationarmy.org.au

Table of Contents

A dream – Introduction 1
Stephen Court (Captain)

Vision 1 – In its entirety 9
Jim Knaggs (Commissioner)

Vision 2 – Sanctified through and through 13
Pam Trigg (Lieut-Colonel)

Vision 3 – Known by this love 19
Carl Schmidtke (Lieut-Colonel)

Vision 4 – Mercy and justice 25
Simon Reeves (Soldier)

Vision 5 – Integrity in expression 31
Wilma Gallet (Soldier)

Vision 6 – The gospel for everyone 35
Aaron Peterson (Soldier)

Vision 7 – Social programs/ eternal effect 41
David Eldridge (Major)

Vision 8 – Eradicate indecencies 49
Danielle Strickland (Captain)

Vision 9 – Biblical social strategy 57
Doug Thomas (Major)

Vision 10 – HQ support 65
    Graeme McClimont (Major)

Vision 11 – Salvo Stores/ E+ = saving stations 71
    Annette Lincoln (Major)

Vision 12 – Salvo Stores/ Trade = Fair Trade 77
    Jean Roper (Soldier)

Vision 13 – Commercial Fair Trade 81
    Sonia Jeffrey (Lieutenant)

Vision 14 – Tracing the lost 87
    Pam Warr (Soldier)

Vision 15 – Adding to our number daily 93
    Bram Southwell (Soldier)

Vision 16 – Growing Army 99
    Doug Davis (Commissioner)

Vision 17 – Pervasive proliferation 105
    Eva Burrows (General Rtd)

Vision 18 – Creative ministry 111
    David Mundy (Major)

Vision 19 – Creative worship 115
    Brian Hogg (Soldier)

Vision 20 – 24/7 prayer 121
    Robert Evans (Captain)

Vision 21 – Lighthouses of prayer 127
 Kirsten Gourd (Soldier)

Vision 22 – Prayer destinations 135
 Frank Daniels (Major)

Vision 23 – Imaginative systems 139
 John Dalziel (Soldier)

Vision 24 – Marked by holiness 145
 Helen Brunt (Major)

Vision 25 – Outpouring of the Spirit 151
 Rowan Castle (Lieutenant)

Vision 26 – Global compassion 155
 K. Brian Morgan (Commissioner)

Vision 27 – Responsive to the voice of God 161
 Fleur Hodge (Soldier)

Vision 28 – Unusual response of the called 167
 Marney Turner (Major)

Vision 29 – The priesthood of all believers 173
 Anthony Castle (Soldier)

Vision 30 – A sparkling, refreshing 'cocktail' 179
 Robyn Clinch (Major)

Vision 31 – Young people filled with the Spirit 185
 Xander Coleman (Soldier)

Vision 32 – Authentic child soldiers 189
    Lisa Wynne (Soldier)

Vision 33 – Extraordinary forgiveness 195
    Barry Gittins (Soldier)

Vision 34 – Love supremely, rely completely 201
    Barbara Wilson (Major)

Vision 35 – Expressing our love 207
    Wesley Harris (Commissioner)

Living the Dream - Conclusion 211
    Jim Knaggs (Commissioner)

SALVO Publishing Catalogue 214

Introduction

Captain Stephen Court

It was the final day of the Aggressive Christianity Conference in Melbourne. ACC had been great, with engaging speakers, important dialogue and significant networking. But God was about to hijack the event.

After sharing a long, involved humorous story and some teaching on our evangelistic role as ambassadors of Christ, without any fanfare, Commissioner Jim Knaggs, our territorial commander, then read the following:

> 'I have a dream that one day The Salvation Army will, in its entirety, be what God wants it to be…
>
> '…that every soldier, young and old, would be sanctified through and through…and out of the passion of their love in Christ, would be an undeniable force for God's love in the world.
>
> '…that this love would be seen between each soldier to demonstrate that God has sent his son into the world not to condemn it, but that the world, through him, might be

saved…and by this would all people know that we are his followers and represent him.

'…that our love would be seen through intentional and overt acts of mercy and justice, all the while in humility before God, not needing to publish our works, only doing them to glorify God.

'…that our mission would have such integrity that every expression of our ministry would be marked not so much by a red shield or even a crest, but by the love of God for people.

'…that every corps would embrace the gospel for everyone in their community, not discriminating by culture, language, social status, or age, and that the helping ministries would be woven into the fabric so that even under a nuclear microscope we could not distinguish between spiritual and social.

'…that every social program would be inviting to any one in need to be helped towards eternal affect, still maintaining our resolve to dispense such love indiscriminately and unconditionally, and that their connections with the corps ministries become seamless to the point that they would become a type of corps in their own right.

'…that we would have effective ministries to eradicate homelessness, human trafficking, prostitution and other indecencies currently common in our society.

'…that our social program strategy will be based upon the needs of people in the context of Biblical mandate, not necessarily the offerings of government contracts.

'…that headquarters' support units would be understood as such, not diminishing their purposes for accountability, but wholly in the context of authentic support and encouragement.

'…that programs such as Salvo Stores and Employment Plus would also become saving stations for the lost and fully integrated into the mission of the territory.

'…that Salvo Stores and the Trade become responsible outlets for Fair Trade goods.

'…that our commercial department at THQ becomes a resource and focal point for facilitating our increasing efforts in Fair Trade.

'…that the Family Tracing Service be expanded to find those souls who have been lost to the Army, assisting in bringing them home, where they belong.

'…that we would never have another day in our existence where someone was not brought to Christ.

'…that our soldiers' roll would only be an increasing reality as would our worship and discipleship meetings.

One Day...

'...that the proliferation of new ministry openings would be so common and normal that we would have to appoint personnel just to keep track of it, most often after the fact.

'...that those gifted with creative ministry gifts would have every opportunity to employ these very skills in the work of the Army.

'...that our worship would be filled with creative means to celebrate God's provisions and presence among us.

'...that our 24/7 Prayer Initiatives will be adopted by individual corps throughout the territory all the time.

'...that we would establish Lighthouses of Prayer to cover our neighbourhoods with grace.

'...that we would have numerous prayer destinations where people could go for prayer retreats, learning opportunities and resources.

'...that our systems would be less restrictive and more imaginative to accommodate the new things God wants to do among us.

'...that as a movement, we would be marked by holiness in corporate and individual praxis.

'…that there would be such an outpouring of the Spirit upon us that we would be courageous and effective witnesses in our families, communities, cities, Australia and the world.

'…that our compassion would be large enough to be understood as authentically global throughout what we do at home and abroad.

'…that our people would be quick to respond to the voice of God for whatever he calls them to.

'…that our officer training programs would be taxed by the unusual response of the called to serve as officers in The Salvation Army.

'…that our local officers would be so empowered to understand their foundational role in the corps ministries and fully embrace the priesthood of all believers.

'…that our women would have appointments and responsibilities commensurate with their gifts, abilities and experience.

'…that our young people would be filled with the spirit and recognised as contributors in the fight.

> '...that our children would be welcomed as authentic soldiers with proper opportunities to celebrate the presence of Christ in their lives and in their environments.
>
> '...that an extraordinary forgiveness and healing of past sins and hurts would prevail upon all people victimised by our practices or inattention.
>
> '...that God would see that we love him supremely through Christ and that our reliance on the Holy Spirit completes his hope in us.
>
> '...that God would see that we love him absolutely and are expressing our love for him by our active love for others.'

I was in the back row. Once the crowd realised that Commissioner Knaggs wasn't reading a simple quote but was downloading a substantial and significant word from the Lord, a spirit of anticipation swept the room as people nudged forward spiritually to the edge of their seats.

The Dream is incendiary. And our response, stage one of which you hold in your hand, has Biblical antecedent:

> 'The Lord answered me: "Write down the vision; write it clearly...so whoever reads it can run to tell others. It is not yet time for the message to come true, but that time is coming

soon; the message will come true. It may seem like a long time, but be patient and wait for it, because it will surely come; it will not be delayed'"

– Habakkuk 2:2,3 (New Century Version)

There are 35 component visions in the Dream. Salvationists from various parts of the territory have generously contributed chapters with their own unique perspectives on the visions. These Salvationists include soldiers and officers, old and young, female and male. They prefigure the broad acceptance and local adaptation of the Dream in towns and cities across Australia. This Dream, though received by Commissioner Knaggs, belongs to the Salvationists of the Territory.

The exigencies of the Salvation War have dictated an approach to this project which benefits from a typical pre-emptory defence loved by primitive Salvos:

> 'Those who may be disposed to criticise this book on its literary demerits, I have no doubt will find ample opportunity, for it has been put together in snatches of time… and under all manner of disadvantages. In this war we have not the time either for the cultivation of the courtesies of life or the elegancies of literature. The great aim with us, in all things, is to do the largest amount of good by the readiest means'
>
> *– William Booth, 1884, The Training of Children*

One Day...

One day... has been designed in such a way that Salvationists in your corps can gather in groups to discuss each vision and how it might be realised on your local front. The brainstorm page following each chapter has been crafted for this purpose.

Pray through the Dream. Brainstorm about the visions. And let each chapter elevate your faith for God to realise his dream for The Salvation Army in Australia Southern Territory and beyond.

Let us speed this day of the Lord, for he seems to be saying, 'I have a dream that one day...'.

From the Territorial Commander

Sis & Dick
―――――――

As I was praying for you today — I recalled I had not yet sent this book —

We trust you are well + that God is blessing you with His abundance.

in christ
Jim

Vision 1 – In its entirety

*"The Salvation Army will in its entirety,
be what God wants it to be…"*

Commissioner Jim Knaggs

In a word, the answer to this hope is holiness…totally immersed in the love of Christ. Seen in God's love for us through Christ, experienced through forgiveness of our sins and provision for life, and expressed through our devotion to our neighbours, we stand as a Salvation Army of love.

Often the military aspect of our composure is seen as a dominating structural vehicle, when in fact, it's better understood as a massive movement of God's people as a force for Him. I believe God wants this understanding from this blessed Army He raised up and continues to lead.

We have taken enough pause to mature as an organisation becoming a trustworthy light in the world. The hour has arrived where we must reaffirm our calling and mission as a people worthy of such a name: The Salvation Army. We must become a flood light of indiscriminate love, boldly and wisely proclaiming healing for the nations and its peoples. Hallelujah!

The entirety of The Salvation Army includes way more than the Australia Southern Territory and stretches to wherever a Salvationist is found. Win the world for Jesus? Win your world for Jesus! Trust God who reminds us that, "The one who calls you is faithful and he will do it." (1 Thessalonians 5:24 (NIV)) It's His call and ours to do in His strength. So I believe His expectation is unlimited as His grace.

The entirety also speaks to the movement itself. Every nook and cranny of the Army needs to be washed in the blood of Jesus, resulting in a truly holy movement to the point where corporate holiness is our standard. While I'm certain this is our intention all over the movement, we need to keep it on the front burner and raise our expectations, never accepting minimalist approaches to communication, employment matters, officer concerns—in fact—in any facet of our ministry.

The entirety includes every corps, social program, every office, every canteen truck, anything with the name, The Salvation Army. This means Salvo Stores and Employment Plus, to name a few more. What does God want for each and every station? He wants it to be deep into His mission, with no excuses for lack of compliance to an aggressive plan of love for others.

Do we really think that we will see success in a treatment or service apart from the influence of God? We won't. God has called us into being and we must have him at the centre of everything we do.

The entirety will include every representative of The Salvation Army, young and old, soldier, employee and volunteer. I do not mean to leave anyone out here. God is inclusive. So should we be. Each one of us, including myself, must be a living witness to the love of God through Christ. Hallelujah!

God wants us to be saved…fully saved and trusting in Him for our lives and our engagement, defeating the enemy at every turn with powerful love in the name of Jesus. Yes!

Be the Army!

Brainstorm:

» Look in the mirror. Do you see what God intended a Salvationist to be? If you can say yes, then we're on our way. If your answer is no, then drop to your knees and give it up to the Lord, who loves you!

» Corps and social programs don't come out of a cookie cutter. What would your corps or program look like if it was what God meant it to be? Building changes? Leadership changes? Clean Sweep? Minor tweaking? These are too easy. Start with who you have and what you've got and get on with it.

» Have you prayed about it? It's the first thing to do. You can start right now.

» Where do you fit in the Army God wants?
   a. You do fit.
   b. It may be right where you are.
   c. It may not be.
   d. He knows.
   e. Ask Him
   f. Do it.

Vision 2 – Sanctified through and through

'…that every soldier, young and old would be sanctified through and through…and out of passion of their love in Christ, would be an undeniable force for God's love in the world.'

Lieutenant-Colonel Pam Trigg

Every December, I take out the Christmas serving dishes from the cupboard to decorate my table and to serve the food. I don't use these dishes at any other time of the year. It's a delight to me when they are set out and used to celebrate this most special occasion. They could be marked 'For Christmas Only'.

In Exodus we read where Moses is directed by God to build the tabernacle. He is given strict instructions for building it, as well as instructions for the furniture. Both the tabernacle and its contents were set apart for God's service. They were sanctified. In Exodus 28:41, Aaron and his sons were sanctified—set apart for the service of the Lord as priests.

Today, some churches set apart vessels and vestments for use in special ceremonies and sacraments of the church. The Salvation Army goes a little further. The 10th doctrine states:

> 'We believe that it is the privilege of all believers to be "wholly sanctified and that their whole spirit and soul and body may be preserved blameless till the coming of our Lord Jesus Christ" (1 Thessalonians 5:23).'

Believe it or not, my Christmas dishes are sanctified for a specific use. To 'sanctify' literally means to set apart for a special use or purpose. The Salvation Army believes that young and old alike can be sanctified—set apart for God.

Those who are sanctified are not only doing things for Christ, they are being like Christ. They are growing into the likeness of Jesus. Often we rush around doing things. Maybe we think people will be impressed with the energy we expend, but being like Christ is allowing Christ and his life to shine through everything we do.

> Christ of Glory, Prince of Peace,
> Let thy life in mine increase;
> Though I live may it be shown
> 'Tis thy life and not my own.
> Dwell within, that men may see
> Christ, the living Christ in me.
>
> *(Colin Fairclough, first verse of song 479,*
> *The Song Book of The Salvation Army)*

Perhaps, like me, you are amazed at the passionate people who have changed our world—people in medicine and science (such as Marie and Pierre Curie, Alexander Fleming, Joseph Lister and Christian Barnard); explorers and adventurers (Christopher Columbus, Robert Scott and Edmund Hilary); people working for justice (Martin Luther King Jr. and Nelson Mandela). These people set themselves apart and, with passion and drive, gave themselves to the world for a purpose. That purpose burned within them as they reached their goal.

The passion of William and Catherine Booth was to reach the down-and-out—Britain's poor and downtrodden—with the gospel of Christ. To many they became Christ. They were passionate, sanctified people and the love they demonstrated was the love of God for all.

Let's face it; it's not easy to love everyone. Sometimes people get under our skin, irritate us or make us uneasy. But we are commanded to love one another. 'Love one another the way I loved you. This is the very best way to love… Remember the root command: Love one another' (John 15, The Message). The only way we know love is learning from Christ's example—he laid down his life for our salvation. Those who are set apart for Christ can be a force in the world today.

One Day...

The Dream sees a time when all believers, young and old, set apart for Christ, are passionate in doing his will to love everyone, no matter who they are. This will become an overpowering force in the world. Can this Dream come true? It depends on us.

Brainstorm:

- » What will The Salvation Army look like when every soldier is sanctified and passionate about bringing the love of Christ to their world?

- » Who is the most passionate person you know? How has he/she changed their world? What is your passion? How will it affect your world?

- » Talk to friends or people in the group about your dream and take note of their responses. Pray for each other's dream.

- » Begin praying for a non-Christian friend. Set yourself apart for them, share your dream with them and be available for them. Share your progress with a friend.

- » Use a concordance, read a book or search the internet and discover your own understanding of 'sanctify'.

- » Pray that God will set you apart and live his life in you.

One Day...

Vision 3 – Known by this love

'…that this love would be seen between each soldier to demonstrate that God has sent his son into the world not to condemn it, but that the world through him might be saved… and by this would all people know that we are his followers and represent him.'

Lieut.-Colonel Carl Schmidtke

Some years ago I was present in a corps meeting when the visiting church growth consultant (a Baptist minister) was asked by a soldier: 'If you were a member in our corps what would be the foundational growth principle that you would seek to put in place?' I remember the pause and then the confident reply: 'I would encourage and nurture a congregation in which we loved each other. Genuinely accepted and loved each other. In our modern society there are so many people looking to experience and belong to a caring and supportive, nurturing community. We wouldn't have to talk about evangelism, or door-knock. They will come to share our experience.'

That reply and the dialogue that followed became a benchmark for my life and my ministry.

I read of a Christian who:

> 'spent a weekend with a Christian ministry for troubled young people. During a morning session of the residents and their parents, a young woman rose to address the group.
>
> With trembling lips and tears of shame streaming down her face, she said, "I've been a prostitute for the last three years. I am so sorry."
>
> As she stood there, paralysed by her vulnerability, her father left his seat, walked to the front of the room, embraced the shaking girl, and said, "When I look at you, I see no prostitute in you. You've been washed. I see my beautiful daughter".
>
> She replied, "I had forgotten the joy of being your little girl"'.[1]

Is it too much of an exaggeration to say each time we slip up, step out of line, fall short of the mark, sin––purposefully, carelessly or even ignorantly––we 'prostitute' ourselves? Sell ourselves?

We need the Father who comes alongside to address us. 'When I look at you, I see no prostitute in you. You've been washed. I see my beautiful child.'

Are these the ongoing words we as a Christian community embrace and 'say' to each other through acceptance, forgiveness,

---

1   Larry Crabb, *Connecting*, (Word Publishing Nashville, Tennessee) p. xviii

love, and kindness in our attitudes and actions? By living-out in community the words of Jesus we testify '...that we are his followers and represent him.'

Thomas Merton wrote, 'Surrender your poverty and acknowledge your nothingness to the Lord. Whether you understand it or not, God loves you, is present in you, lives in you, dwells in you, calls you, saves you and offers you an understanding and compassion which are like nothing you have ever found in a book or heard in a sermon.'[1]

William Booth spoke many years ago, at the launch of a new translation of the Bible that we (Salvationists/Christians) are the translation of the Bible that people will read.

Therefore, Booth is echoing the words of Jesus. 'Let me give you a new command: Love one another. In the same way I loved you, you love one another. This is how everyone will recognize that you are my disciples––when they see the love you have for each other' (John 13.34-35 *The Message*).

---

1 Quoted by Brennan Manning in '*The Rabbi's Heartbeat*', Navpress 2003 – from *The Hidden Ground of Love; Letters*, (New York; Farrar, Strauss, Giroux, 1985) p.146

I have German heritage. My parents were Salvation Army Officers in Germany before serving in China and Australia, following migration. They were commissioned as officers of the 'Heils Armee', which translates to, 'Healing Army'. I discovered that 'Salvation' and 'Healing' originate from the same root word. In fact, an early translator of the Bible used the word 'Healing' throughout scripture.

Is this not 'The Dream'? That our corps, congregations, community centres are the 'healing army' of Jesus––living out together the on-going healing word of God within us and our wider community.

Brainstorm:

- In a group discuss John 13:34-35 and your corps/centre. Consider:
  a. Strengths
  b. Weaknesses
  c. Opportunities
  d. Trends

- What outcomes should we aim for to realise 'The Dream'?

- What steps will we put into place to achieve the outcomes.

- In a group:
  a. Distribute sheets of paper to each member. Each person to draw a line-map of their life's journey including high points and low points.
  b. In turn share with group some of the high and low points.
  c. In smaller groups or with a partner, pray for each other (or pledge support to each other).

- Personally or in a small group explore with a Bible concordance the references to 'love' from John's Gospel. (This can also be done on the internet through such sites as www.biblegateway.com)

a. If personally––reflect on each passage and apply to self.
  b. In group––reflect, then in turn, each share one passage: '(This passage)… is saying to me…'

» Reflect and discuss the comment––'Is it too much of an exaggeration to say… we prostitute ourselves?'
  a. Why?
  b. How may we experience forgiveness?
  c. How may we affirm each other on our journey?

» If we are a 'Healing Army' how do we apply it in our group/centre?
  a. What are the outcomes (goals) we want to achieve?
  b. What steps should we put into place?
  c. How will we recognise that we are achieving the steps and outcomes?

Vision 4 – Mercy and justice

'…that our love would be seen through intentional and overt acts of mercy and justice, all the while in humility before God, not needing to publish our works, only doing them to glorify God'.

Simon Reeves

There is a sign above our front door that says, 'Today…small things with great love (or don't open the door)'. This sign reminds us that we are not God, we cannot save the whole world. Salvationists, often with a heart for social justice, face the danger of trying to save the whole world. Even though this is a noble endeavor it can sometimes be motivated unconsciously by our own ego seeking 'greatness'. Alternatively, the 'save the world' complex may lead to burnout and disillusionment.

The truth is, however, that it is Jesus Christ who saves the world and he did that on the cross. The reign of God is at hand. So, when we accept the salvation of Jesus, what then is our role? Our role is to show that the world has indeed been saved. The Salvation Army and all its soldiers exist to embody the reign of God and to live out its reality.

How do we do that? We engage in intentional and overt acts of mercy and justice, not to save the world, not to please our egos, but because this is whom we have become by following Jesus. Mercy and justice become the air we breathe.

Yet, the message we receive from the nations of the world seems to be: 'Blessed are you who create and benefit from injustice. Blessed are those who show no mercy towards others. To the poor, homeless, refugees, Bali bombers, pedophiles, Iraqis, or anyone who does wrong to us—no mercy'.

Jesus says, in the kingdom of God, 'Blessed are those who hunger and thirst for justice' and 'blessed are the merciful' (Matthew 5:6–7). To hunger and thirst is to daily seek justice as we would food and drink. Doing justice is not one great thing we do once in our lives, or when we put on a uniform or when we clock on at our social centre, it is a normal, daily existence. It is doing small daily acts with great love.

We can look to Jesus who lived doing justice daily, at mealtimes, commuting, talking in the market place, at weddings or labouring in fields. We are to do the same. But a warning! Justice will disturb our lives. Justice will wake us up at night to a knock on the door from the homeless, take us to the streets to speak out against war and cause disagreements with our friends over dinner. Justice may get us killed, but we wouldn't be the first!

While justice is pursued, we equally seek mercy. Mercy is what makes justice real. If we cannot offer mercy to our own family, friends, neighbours, and especially those who've hurt us, then we cannot rightly pursue justice. Jesus puts anger on a par with murder, and instructs us to forgive one another millions of times over. Thomas Merton described God as 'Mercy within mercy within mercy'.

However, Jesus doesn't stop there. He says we are even to show mercy and love to our enemies! Here is the most radical and revolutionary statement made in human history. Can he be serious? Maybe the question is how seriously do we follow Jesus?

Each of us has the potential for mercy or no mercy, to work for justice or create injustice, to save a life or kill. This is the most frightening part of our humanity, but also the one that gives us the most hope. We are to do justice and seek mercy because of who we are, individually and as The Salvation Army. We do so in humility, whether or not our works will be published. To glorify God and say that the kingdom of God is at hand.

Jesus has shown us the way and lives today.

Brainstorm:

Justice

We can all work on one or two projects for justice and peace. Choose one local issue and one global issue.

» Who lives next door to you? What injustices do they face
» Claim the end of injustice and live out its future. Never look back until it has come to pass.

> A future where everyone is paid a fair wage
> A future where everyone has a home
> A future where everyone has enough food and drink
>
> A future of clean, renewable sources of energy
> A future without war
> A future where everyone has work
> A future where no one is ever lonely again

» Read about futures that have come to pass. Learn from their stories:
   a. Gandhi and the nonviolent liberation of India
   b. Nelson Mandela and apartheid
   c. Martin Luther King Jr and segregation
   d. William Wilberforce and slavery

Mercy
- » How do we grow in mercy?
- » How has the unending mercy of God in your life led you to have unending mercy for others?

- » Some ideas
    a. Meditate and pray:
       Read the Sermon on the Mount everyday for the rest of your life. In these three chapters lies all you need for a life of mercy and love.
    b. Learn to fit the stories of Jesus into the stories of your life.
    c. Open up your homes to strangers—one of the greatest tests of mercy.
    d. Spend time with people who the media and society say are 'worthless' and 'undeserving'.
    e. Value people over possessions.

- » Reading
    a. *Say to this Mountain*, Ched Myers
    b. *Jesus the Rebel*, John Dear
    c. *The Irresistible Revolution*, Shane Claiborne
    d. *The Powers that Be*, Walter Wink

30 One Day...

Vision 5 – Integrity in expression

'...that our mission would have such integrity that every expression of our ministry would be marked not so much by a red shield or even a crest, but by the love of God for people.'

Wilma Gallet

God's love for people is unconditional; it is beyond measure. God loves with an aching heart; his very essence is love. Scripture tells us, 'This is how God showed his love among us; He sent his one and only son into the world that we might live through him. This is love: not that we loved God but that he loved us and sent his son as an atoning sacrifice for our sins. Dear friends, since God so loved us, we also ought to love one another...If we love one another, God lives in us and his love is made complete in us' (1 John 4: 9–12).

Loving others should be a natural response to God's love for us and we demonstrate this through acts of loving kindness and practical concern for one another's well being.

Jesus shows us what this might look like in the story of the Good Samaritan. The response of the Samaritan in this unforgettable picture of a man, who had been robbed, beaten and left for dead is the embodiment of love in action. Priestly and respectable men hurried past the man in distress, in fear of their own lives and reputation, but the Samaritan—paying no heed for his own safety—acted out of a heart of compassion and did everything that was necessary to save the man's life.

This is the response Jesus requires of all who follow him. He calls us to love the Lord God and to love our neighbour. Our mission, and every expression of Salvation Army ministry and service, is to be a natural outpouring of this love. Giving out of a heart of love means setting aside prejudices and judgemental opinions. It means giving because the other person has a need and not expecting anything in return.

The Salvation Army is renowned for its ministry of service and professional social work. All of this must be driven by love for our neighbour. It's out of this sense of care for our neighbour that we give and serve—not out of organisational or professional pride and or because we want to grow and expand—but simply because there is a great depth of human need which only the love of God for people can fill.

Our mission must be hallmarked by this love, it sets us apart and people should feel the difference whether they work for The Salvation Army, worship with us or come to us with needs.

There are many people within our community who have struggles in life, who are confronted with daily challenges. Sometimes this is a result of poor choices or decisions, sometimes it's a result of injustices and/or an unjust system. All people regardless of their circumstances are deserving of unconditional love and respect. We need to examine our hearts to see if we demonstrate God's love in all of our actions and to see if we love not only those people we can identify with, but also those who oppose us—those who challenge our sensibilities, people who don't share our views, our values, our lifestyle choices.

We are commanded to 'Love one another just as I have loved you'—this is not an optional extra. As followers of Jesus we are to demonstrate God's love for people in word and deed. This means loving everyone, not just our friends and families but those we find difficult to love. When we serve from a heart of love we see the inner beauty in every individual. We see their inherent worth and the profound spark of the Divine in every created being.

Brainstorm:

» There are many lonely and isolated people in every community. Corps can become active in providing a sense of community and belonging for people by acting out of a heart of love. For example:

a. *Care for refugees*

 There are many refugees in Australia, whose visa status is Bridging Visa E. This means that while they wait for the Department of Immigration to process their claim, they have no access to benefits or employment. These people live with fear and uncertainty everyday. They need friendship and support. Local corps could respond with:
 - Outreach visits
 - Meals/friendship club
 - Conversational English
 - Sporting activities

b. *Caring for people bereaved by suicide*

 The Salvation Army Hope for Life web based training programs will provide resources and training to help corps reach out to people bereaved by suicide.

c. *Care for people who are economically disadvantaged*
 - Meals programs, particularly a weekly lunch
 - Impromptu outings

Vision 6 – The gospel for everyone

'…that every corps would embrace the gospel for everyone in their community, not discriminating by culture, language, social status, or age…and that the helping ministries would be woven into the fabric so that even under a nuclear microscope we could not distinguish between spiritual and social.'

Aaron Peterson

The instructions are simple: act justly, love mercy and walk humbly with your God (Micah 6:8).

The implication is that a Christian life involves more than just a relationship with God; it also involves deep relationships with other people. When I first read these words it awakened in me a realisation that the impact of the gospel extended beyond my corps, beyond a group of people who are just like me.

Discovering that the gospel was not the exclusive domain of Australia's white, educated, middle class was akin to Alice entering the rabbit's hole. With each new step came experiences that were paradoxically unsettling and reassuring. New experiences challenged the established paradigms of Christian life and culture that existed within my mind. I was also relieved to discover that the gospel was far richer than I had first thought.

When Jesus spoke of the fulfilment of Isaiah's prophecy he said, 'The Spirit of the Lord is upon me because he has anointed me to preach the good news to the poor. He has sent me to proclaim freedom for the prisoners and recovery of sight to the blind, to release the oppressed, to proclaim the year of the Lord's favour.'

Yet Jesus was not speaking exclusively in literal terms. We know this because he spoke the gospel into people's lives without discriminating by culture, language, social status or age. Jesus proclaimed the good news as powerfully to the social elite—the Sanhedrin, the Pharisees and the occupying Roman forces—as he did to the social outcasts—women, the lame and criminals.

Sin does not discriminate by culture, language, social status or age. Neither should our preaching of the good news.

But the gospel must consist of more than just words. When a Christian does nothing but talk about what must be done to experience a life with Christ the message of the gospel sounds more like good advice than good news.

Our movement has a wonderful tradition of bringing the holistic gospel to all people—a gospel that is based upon the dual pillars of faith and works. But with the increased professionalising of practical ministries within The Salvation Army we risk devaluing the gospel by divorcing the temporal and spiritual elements.

I've not seen many examples of true incarnational corps. There have been individuals who have brought the gospel to their community with the social and spiritual components perfectly interwoven. But never had I seen such a venture achieved systematically until I travelled to The Salvation Army's Guatemala division.

Soldiering at the Mesketal Corps is a dangerous proposition. Gun battles among gangs are commonplace, officers have been kidnapped and there are two bullet holes in the front door.

I had the privilege of spending some time with Mariela, a teacher at the primary school operated at the corps. She is also a soldier at Mesketal Corps and takes responsibility for running the junior soldier program here four nights per week and helps out with Sunday school. When junior soldiers finishs each night, it is Mariela's job to walk the kids home after dark through Mesketal's gun riddled streets.

If you are struggling to find a means to integrate social and spiritual ministries, then turn to Guatemala as a case study. Mariela's role as a Salvationist is to provide spiritual and educational guidance to the children of her neighbourhood. Yet her roles are so intertwined with one another it is hard to see where one starts and the other stops.

Her ministry is not restricted to the hours of her program, but it runs through every aspect of her life. Mariela's lifestyle is a true reflection of God living in a community.

Brainstorm:

- How long does it take to get to your corps?
- Do you know people who live near your corps?
- Is your job a form of ministry?
- Do you use words to speak of the gospel?
- Do you use actions to speak of the gospel?
- Are the spiritual and social ministries at your corps woven together in a seamless fabric?

One Day...

Vision 7 – Social programs / eternal effect

'…that every social program would be inviting to any one in need to be helped towards eternal affect, still maintaining our resolve to dispense such love indiscriminately and unconditionally…and that their connections with the corps ministries become seamless to the point that they would become a type of corps in their own right.'

Major David Eldridge

The Salvation Army is one of the largest providers of community support in Australia. Every day, thousands of Australians turn to the Army and receive timely and effective assistance. While our primary focus is on the most marginalised people, we respond to those from any social background requiring our practical support.

Some years ago, Brian Burdekin, the Federal Human Rights and Equal Opportunities Commissioner, was speaking at a dinner about youth homelessness. During this speech he shared his feelings about the uniqueness of The Salvation Army's social work. He said that what he appreciated most was that we delivered 'programs that valued the worth of the human soul'. This was, and is, an astute observation—which captures something of what is special about Salvation Army programs.

Australians believe that everybody deserves a 'fair go'. This concern is deeply embedded in our national culture and psyche. The Salvation Army has a high approval rating in the community because we are seen to be sharing and practising this ethos. For most Australians, actions speak louder than words. We have been blessed with officers, soldiers and employees who have risen to the challenge of helping people, resolving social problems and battling against social evils with sacrificial dedication.

Today, social work demands higher standards of professional skill because it operates in a more complex social environment. A contemporary reality is that there are not enough qualified Salvationists to staff our extensive network of social programs. Consequently, many of our employees do not share our religious convictions. However, in the main we have been able to recruit exceptional people who, although they may not necessarily share our religious convictions, they do share our values and our practical commitment to 'alleviating human need without discrimination'. They work with us to transform lives broken by a combination of individual and family tragedies as well as social and economic disadvantage.

People come to us with a wide range of issues. Most come when they are experiencing acute crises. Initially, our skilled social program staff are focused on crisis resolution—whether that involves homelessness, addictions, mental illness, violence or abuse. However, our help should go further and offer new hope and a way forward. Beyond crisis, our work must build social support networks so that people can live good lives in communities that care. This will only be achieved where there is a continuum of opportunities from an intentional transition out of crisis through to engagement in mainstream community life.

Our early social work was so inclusive of people deemed 'undeserving' that we were often in conflict with other social agencies. This conflict was a necessary consequence of our priority commitment to social work programs that were inviting, accessible, compassionate and indiscriminate in their care for people. The mission of The Salvation Army has always been, is, and should always be, to set aside prejudice and judgmental attitudes to engage directly with people at their point of need. This remains a primary imperative for our corps and social programs.

An aspirational goal set by the Australia Southern Territory for both corps and social programs is the building of 'belonging communities'. Achieving this goal requires an intentional commitment to meet the expressed needs of people by offering genuine opportunities for life changing transformation. While it is true that some people still experience 'Damascus Road' transformations, it is more often the case that lasting change is built on relational and faith encounters along the path of a lifelong journey of personal and spiritual growth. The 'belonging community' is critical for this journey. In their book, The Shaping of Things To Come, Michael Frost and Alan Hirsch affirm that 'people today are searching for relational communities that offer belonging, empowerment, and redemption.'

In parts of our territory, we have achieved an integrated mission approach that enables people to address life crises and then move into corps networks where there is personal support and developmental activities. Some social programs support people for an extended period and this allows time for engagement in recreation programs, social activities and an opportunity for chaplains to work on spiritual issues. However, many social programs are only funded for short-term interventions and are unable to work with people for long enough to connect them to corps or other community supports. Therefore, not all corps are able to link up with the people involved with our social programs and not all social programs can connect with people for sufficient time to enable significant change.

In order to realise any dream of holistic social service, and a seamless integration of corps and social programs, we need to prayerfully and thoughtfully engage with the people who use our services and respect the complexity of their lives. The incarnational model of Jesus Christ's journey with his followers—referred to by Swinburne University's Professor David MacKenzie as 'bodily praxis'—shows a way of understanding how Salvation Army ministry can best serve those who come to us. Jesus set out on a journey with his friends with a deep understanding of their culture. It was a journey that was about growth, redemption and liberation.

To live incarnationally, corps and social programs need to be listening and belonging communities that embody the healing and redemptive ministry of The Salvation Army. A ministry available to any person with physical, emotional or spiritual needs.

Brainstorm:

Where better to find quotes that challenge our thinking about the character of the compassionate care of Salvation Army ministry than in the words of William Booth, one of our founders. Setting aside the non-inclusive language of Victorian England, the quotes given below are worth reflecting on.

> 'Here is one of the foundation principles of our social work. From the beginning we have said openly that our love and labour are for all. It is not necessary to have a good character to secure our compassion and help. We do not make it a condition of being blessed and comforted that a man should belong to a union or go to a church or join The Salvation Army. We make, so far as we can, our sun, like our Father's, to shine on what are called the "undeserving", the "worthless" poor as well as on the others; and our rain to descend on the bad and idle, as well as on the good and industrious.'

Given a growing tendency in Australian society to 'blame the victim' and use terms such as 'dole bludger' and 'illegal immigrants', is now the time to stand beside the poor and demand justice and the often talked about 'fair go for all'?

> 'But what is the use of preaching the gospel to men whose whole attention is concentrated upon a mad, desperate struggle to keep themselves alive? You might as well give a tract to a

shipwrecked sailor who is battling the surf which has drowned his comrades and threatens to drown him. He will not listen to you. Nay, he cannot hear you any more than a man whose head is under water can listen to a sermon. The first thing to do is to get him at least a footing on firm ground and to give him room to live. Then you may have a chance. At present you have none.'

How do people find a way forward from the despair of poverty, abuse and crushed self-esteem? What role can Salvation Army corps and social programs play in helping people find 'a footing on firm ground'?

'Why all this apparatus of temples and meeting houses to save men from perdition in a world which is to come, while never a helping hand is stretched out to save them from the inferno of their present life'?

What do you think church should be like in 21st century Australia? How can we build inclusive and non-judgemental faith communities that are consistent with the teachings of Jesus?

One Day...

Vision 8 – Eradicate Indecencies

> *'…that we would have effective ministries to eradicate homelessness, human trafficking, prostitution and other indecencies currently common in our society.'*
>
> *Captain Danielle Strickland*

When Jesus taught his disciples to pray he told them to pray, 'Our Father who art in heaven… Your Kingdom come, your will be done on earth as it is in heaven.'

That's a powerful prayer—and an even more amazing thought.

For years the Christian church and, dare I say even The Salvation Army, has had a 'survivor' posture. We thought if we huddled together and stayed 'holy' inside the church, perhaps we'd be safe from the evil that permeated every aspect of the world. After all, the 'devil prowls around like a lion'.

Perhaps spurred on by the 'pre-millennial rapture' theory (if we hang on tight Jesus will zap us out of here before the real disaster), we bought the lie that the world would infect us with sin, and missed the essential truth of the gospel message—the Kingdom is for now.

One Day...

Jason Upton (a worship leader) used to say that everywhere he went people were praying for an open heaven. He suggests heaven has been open since Jesus returned—what we should be praying for is an open earth.

Infectious holiness—one that is radically based in the gospels—is one that infects the earth. We are called to be light and salt. We are born to be influencers—world changers and shapers.

Catherine Booth used to tuck her children into bed every night and remind them that they were going to change the world. I wish as spiritual children of that mother we'd turn our ear to overhear! We are called to advance God's kingdom (where every wrong is put right) on the earth.

The Word says that the gates of hell cannot stop the advancing kingdom of God on the earth. Every great revival was accompanied by great social reform. Our own radical history was a social scheme birthed out of laying hold of the kingdom and bringing it to earth.

Every great social reformer had tasted heaven. Even Gandhi admitted that in his amazing social movement to free India all he really did was put the words of Jesus into action.

What I like about this dream is that it's aggressively kingdom-focused. God doesn't just want to make a dent in poverty; he wants to eradicate it. He doesn't want only one prostitute welcomed into community and redeemed; he wants the oppression of prostitution to be removed. He wants the systemic realities of evil (the human slave trade, economic prejudices, war and refugees) to be dismantled and righteous ones raised up in their place.

When economics expert Jeffery Sachs writes about the end of poverty he believes that with applied effort we can see extreme poverty wiped out in this current generation.

Mohammad Yaris, after receiving the Nobel Peace Prize this year (2007) for his amazing micro-enterprise bank for the developing world, said he believes his grandchildren will have to go to a museum to see extreme poverty.

These are dreamers, but how beautiful the dream, for it's not a new one, it's an ancient one—the dream of Heaven itself. This dream is echoed in the pages of scripture and in the prayers of the saints for generations. It's time to see clearly now.

This kingdom vision says, 'Your kingdom come, Your will be done on earth as it is in heaven'. And it is happening right now. God's kingdom is coming—join in!

I believe, with Commissioner Knaggs, that this generation of Salvationists will rise up and fight for the advance of the kingdom of heaven.

It looks like the Spirit of the Lord upon every willing and obedient soldier empowering them to preach good news to the poor, bind up the broken captive, release the prisoners and heal the blind.

It looks like government advocacy, brothel chaplaincy, rescue homes for trafficked victims; it looks like every quarters becoming a mission station for the poor; and it looks like every soldier living in direct contrast to the ways of the world, leaving behind lives of excess for simplicity in order to celebrate kingdom generosity!

It looks messy, dirty, colourful and free. It looks like long days and short nights full of prayer and then the obedience to get up off our knees to advance the war. It looks like right now. Can you hear heaven's heartbeat in the rhythm of the Dream itself?

This is good news. Join in. We are not fighting flesh and blood but principalities and powers in the spiritual realm. William Booth said Salvationism was simply this: the overcoming and banishing from the earth of wickedness.

God grant it. Now to live the Dream.

One Day...

Brainstorm:

Some campaigns already started:

The fair trade principle. In action right now. The Salvation Army in Australia recognises its potential (both as an example and a consumer) to consume fairly. In our coffee, tea and chocolate consumption, we can make a difference in the lives of some of the world's poorest people. As an organisation we are convinced it's time we led the way to new economic strategies to help relieve poverty in the world.

What if every Salvationist determined to buy fair trade? We could make a huge difference in the way people live (both those in the developing world and the developed world) and give the world the truth, 'there is nothing like an Army cup of tea!'

JUSTLose:
The thing that causes the most slavery in the world is our excesses (coffee, chocolate and sex are three of them, but there are many more). Those same things that enslave people physically are the very things that enslave us as well (obesity and desire). We are rising up as the people of God to say 'No' to excess so that others can be literally freed. Join the campaign today!

What if 100 Salvationists led teams of ten to confront the cultural disease of excess? Could we free thousands and effect change the world over?

JUSTPray:
Freedom Fridays: Salvationists called to fast and pray every Friday at noon, asking God for his help to end the sexual slavery of thousands of young women and children.

JUSTLive:
Salvationists hearing the call of our roots to re-establish the 'slum sisters and brothers' movement of our beginnings—called to incarnate themselves among the poor, as Jesus did.

Imagine the worst 100 post codes being invaded by light-bearers and God's people bringing hope into the darkest places!

How about mobilised grassroots movements that determine to shape the policies instead of react to them (affordable housing, addictions, indigenous communities, refugees and poverty rates both within Australia and around the world).

Every Salvationist home open to the 'stranger' and 'alien'—a refugee family relocated and embraced by the community of God.

One Day...

Vision 9 – Biblical social strategy

'…that our social program strategy will be based upon the needs of people in the context of Biblical mandate, not necessarily the offerings of government contracts.'

Major Doug Thomas

The Salvation Army is one of Australia's major providers of government funded social and welfare services. It is estimated that The Salvation Army provides 25 percent of services of the government-funded housing and homelessness sector in Victoria. We are also major players in drug and alcohol services, placement and support services for at-risk children and young people, aged care (still), prison chaplaincy, Job Network employment services, and the delivery of emergency relief.

In Melbourne Central Division about 80 percent of our $45 million annual social program operating budget is from government funding. Of the remainder, about 75 percent is mission funding through the Red Shield Appeal, while the rest consists mainly of client fee-for-service.

Unequal partnership with government:
Government and service providers form a partnership of sorts. The government department acts as if it is the senior partner, contracting for service provision from the service providers (purchaser/provider relationship). The government controls the allocation of funds, but they also determine the underlying service values and policy, the service type, the target group and decide the hoped for outcomes.

For their part, the service providers submit tenders, often in competition with one another, provide the infrastructure (suitably qualified and experienced staff, premises, vehicles, IT services, and business organisation etc), and submit regular reports to the funding body to demonstrate they are meeting their contractual obligations. There are situations where experienced staff maybe invited to the policy table or the program development table, but this is, most definitely, not a partnership between equals.

'Soup, soap and salvation':
More than 50 years ago, Abraham Maslow published his well-known theory of motivation, popularly known as Maslow's Hierarchy of Needs. According to Maslow, there exists in each person a hierarchy of five need levels (physiological, safety, social, esteem, and self-actualisation), and each level must be substantially satisfied before the next level need becomes

dominant. Provided altruism and vocation are both conveniently ignored, there is something intuitive about his model for explaining what drives people.

Some 60 years prior to Maslow, another social practitioner postulated a simpler three level 'hierarchy of needs'. William Booth's 'Soup, Soap and Salvation' cannot be definitely sourced, but John Philip Sousa referred to it in his eulogy for the Founder, and it has certainly become part of the Army's folklore. This catchphrase still defines the Army's engagement with the kingdom of the world in order to help build the kingdom of God.

'Soup' represents all a person's physiological needs—food, shelter, clothing, safety and security. William Booth is reported to have said that it is of no use to preach to a man who has an empty stomach.

'Soap' represents psycho-social-emotional wellbeing, and anything that brings a person dignity. People who are conscious of their own uncleanness or sense of inadequacy, or who cause others to shy away from them, can regard themselves as inferior and are therefore not in a position to engage in relationships or community.

'Salvation' represents right relationship and peace with God through having dealt with the past through the blood of Jesus; through having spiritual power, meaning and purpose for the present life, and through holding hope for the future. This is self-actualisation at its highest.

In order to be true to itself, The Salvation Army must engage with people in a way that is truly holistic. Any factor which puts a limitation on our activities—resource limitation, lack of commitment or passion amongst our personnel, or restricted program or service targets—causes us to do something less than our best possible work.

Biblical mandate:
The Christian church operates under a number of different Biblical mandates. There is the Great Commission ('Go into all the world and preach the gospel,' Matthew 28:18–20). There is Jesus' teaching on the sheep and the goats ('Whatever you did for the least of these brothers of mine, you did for me,' Matthew 25:31–46). There is Christ's teaching on the two greatest commandments ('Love God…love your neighbour as yourself' which acted to the prologue to Jesus' well-loved parable of the Good Samaritan in Luke 10:25–37). There is also much teaching in the tradition of the Old Testament prophets that identified the

fatherless, widows and aliens as people especially under God's protection (Deuteronomy 10:18 and others).

These different mandates are not in conflict with one another, but represent different focuses in response to particular circumstances. Clearly there is mandate here for The Salvation Army's holistic approach to mission and ministry.

The Dream:

There is massive community expectation on The Salvation Army that we will continue to deliver our services to people in need. Also, we are a major employer, and we have a responsibility to our existing staff. It is unlikely that we could ever walk away from the delivery of government-funded programs, and certainly not in the near future.

However we must take ownership of our mission and ensure that we remain true to our Biblical mandates, providing services that are truly holistic, and where we intentionally seek out people who are overlooked or have proven too difficult for other services.

We can continue to allow the government to provide core-funding and then must surround this with mission funding which allows us to 'value-add':

- To work, where necessary, with people for longer or more intensively than stipulated in the government contract;

- To accept people from outside the direct catchment area if otherwise appropriate;

- To go beyond just addressing the person's 'presenting needs';

- To ensure that every person has the opportunity to explore their spiritual issues with someone who can appropriately and articulately share the good news of the gospel with them;

- To provide clear linkages into sustaining supportive communities, such as corps;

- To use our client data, practice wisdom and sheer 'mass' as a foundation for policy and program development in partnership with government, for advocacy on social issues, and eventually, for the reform of society.

Brainstorm:

What can you do?

- » Promote the Red Shield Appeal as the source of mission funding. Participate at a local level—every dollar counts!
- » Get to know your local social services network or program. Try to befriend and demonstrate that you value our passionate and highly committed staff.
- » Ensure that any people who are referred to your corps are followed up and made to feel welcome, though not 'exhibits at an exhibition'. Be sensitive.
- » Identify young people at your corps who have an interest in taking on tertiary studies in the human services (social work, welfare, youth work, psychology, alcohol and drug work). Encourage them and inform them of The Salvation Army's social internship program that is able to support them throughout their studies.
- » Ask your corps officer to invite someone from a social program to come and address the corps. We are all working to the one mission.
- » Register as a volunteer. Commit to any required training.

One Day...

Vision 10 – HQ support

'…that headquarters units would be understood as such [support units], not diminishing their purposes for accountability, but wholly in the context of support and encouragement.'

Major Graeme McClimont

The words, 'I'm from THQ and I'm here to help you' strike an uneasy note for those who are directly involved, face-to-face, in delivering the mission. Technical experts who fly in, complete a training course, carry out a review and fly out don't carry the weight of battle on their shoulders and organisational bureaucrats disconnected from the fight by distance and years driving desks can be immune from the rigours of the struggle.

People at the forefront of mission need to know they are valued and respected, that there are those who care for them and pray for them, and that there are those who can be trusted for assistance, genuine advice and mentoring. Can they obtain all of this from their DHQ or THQ?

At present one in every four officers is appointed to either THQ or DHQ. In an increasingly complex world the functional demands placed upon The Salvation Army have grown exponentially. Time, resources and personnel are sucked into a seemingly irresistible vortex that has no end and the burden of many of these functions is experienced at the forefront of mission in terms of added paper work and increasingly slow and confusing bureaucratic processes.

A territorial commander of one of the most rapidly growing territories in the Army world was heard to remark that the growth of the Army was inversely proportional to the size of THQ (i.e. as THQs get bigger, the Army gets smaller).

Perhaps, in Jesus' time, it was the lawyers, the scribes and, of course, the Pharisees who occupied the place that church bureaucrats and administrators occupy today.

Jesus had extreme trouble with them, not so much because they were bad people but because they were resistant to change and they assumed a place of importance bestowed on them by culture. They were concerned for the letter of the law rather than the spirit of the law and perceived themselves as the keepers of tradition. It was perhaps the inflexible abuse of authority that caused Jesus to be so angry with them and he was a definite threat to their control and respectable way of life.

May our DHQs and THQs never reach such a barren place. If, however, they become so focused on their own internal processes they become self-serving and take on a life of their own. Then these headquarters would become largely disconnected from the mission and fail to support in the way they should.

Headquarters units must see their role in terms of support rather than control. Encouragement rather than authority is essential in order to best provide support to battle-weary and battle-hardened Christian soldiers. Whether we work at the forefront of mission or in headquarters, there is a need for each of us to see ourselves as colleagues in Christ. We are all involved in the same mission.

Perhaps one of the ways we can overcome the tendency to 'bureaucratise' things is to arrange for a direct mission appointment for every officer who serves on THQ and DHQ. This would involve each officer in mission for a day, or half a day, each week and, as an appointment, it would be a task and ministry for which they are accountable. The officer would benefit by being connected to the mission and it would impact upon their performance at THQ or DHQ.

Accountability, usually seen as a function of administration and management, can perhaps be seen slightly differently within the Army—more as a two-way, rather than a one-way process. If we are colleagues in Christ, then surely the soldier at the forefront of mission should have the same opportunity to enquire of the person at headquarters as does the person at headquarters to enquire of the soldier.

An additional problem as THQs and DHQs grow (and the demands become more complex) is the inclusion of a range of professional roles that can bring with them the values of the marketsquare—power, greed and competition. When values such as these are woven into the professional frameworks of employees, they can constitute a significant challenge to a Christian organisation, particularly when these values are foundational to accountability requirements.

In this increasingly complex and demanding world we dream of a day when all who work at the battlefront will be able to say, 'I can do what I have to do because I know that God in Christ walks beside me and he walks beside those who encourage me and support me at DHQ and THQ. I can trust them, I can lean on them, I can be challenged by them, yet know I am respected and genuinely loved. They are praying with me and for me.'

Brainstorm:

Through another's eyes:

Some scholars tell us that the story from John 8 (where Jesus challenges the hypocrisy of those who would condemn a woman caught in the very act of adultery) is a later insertion and not part of the original text. The story does however have the strong ring of the gospel of Jesus Christ about it. We can easily picture Jesus as he challenges bad attitudes, beliefs and behaviour. We can also look through the eyes of those present on that occasion and take their perspective in prayer—the perspective of a Pharisee, bystander, the woman herself and, finally, we can look through the eyes of Jesus himself.

Prayer - Through another's eyes

> It's easy to be a bystander,
> To allow the events of life to pass us by,
> To select the moment but not to get involved,
> To enjoy the spectacle and then to move on,
> To protect my private world and know that I am safe.
>
> It takes courage to be a pharisee,
> To engage in the difficult tasks of religion and rule,
> To keep the precepts but to remain human,

One Day...

To maintain strict justice and to keep oneself pure,
To ensure our world is right and does not change.

It's hard to be a sinner,
To look friends in the face when our wrongdoing is uncovered,
To accept the judgement but know that others not judged are even more guilty,
To cope with the fear and retain dignity intact,
To maintain hope, and hope to live again.

Can we look through the eyes of Christ,
And see the brokenness in a human soul?
To comprehend the injustice in the heart of the self-righteous,
The indifference in the mindless crowd.

Lord grant me grace that I might see though your eyes
Let me be aware of my own folly and sin
Knowing my judgmental attitudes and prejudice
That I might act with compassion and understanding
Transparently reflecting in my life the love you have for me.

Discuss!

Should all THQ and DHQ officers have an additional part-time mission appointment?

Vision 11 – Salvo Stores / E+ = saving stations

'I have a dream, that one day programs such as Salvos Stores and Employment Plus would also become saving stations for the lost and fully integrated into the mission of the territory.'

Major Annette Lincoln

(editor's note: read this chapter as if you were reading the *Narnia* series or *The Lord of the Rings*).

I have a dream, in seven episodes, that proceeds like a trickle out of the temple—the house of sacrifice and worship, the place where grace runs down like blood from the altar, onto the floor and then out the door until it touches the common man who is mending his nets, building his business or crafting his wares.

Those standing around the altar are the first to be touched by the drops, and they begin to lift their arms in praise to the lamb, for they have seen a vision of amazing grace. In praise and thankfulness they are lifted to a place where they can see the wonders of 'a truly blessed life'.

Episode 1. The corps officer silently wonders, 'If I failed to grow my congregation by 5% each year, my job wouldn't be on the line. This group of people has supported me through thick and thin, even when I constantly fail. That struggling Salvo store manager down there is not as blessed in the same way as I am. God, I want to help, guide me towards offering what little I can give. Please show me what to do'.

Episode 2. Meanwhile, the corps realises that God blesses and multiplies gifts and accepts and uses sacrifices. And they notice that many outside the congregation have contributed. Some of the workers in the nearest Salvos store and E Plus have hearts touched by God to labour for such a 'a worthy cause' (which is in reality, that of the corps).

Episode 3. In the midst of the worship, one soldier hears these words in her heart––'In as far as you did it to one of the least of these my brethren, you did it to me.'

Armed with the gift of encouragement she leaves worship for the Salvo store, finds the manager and says, 'I've never been to this shop before and that has been my loss, I want to say thank you for the wonderful work you do. You and all your staff and volunteers have enabled us to do so much good. Thank you for the money you raise; it has really helped The Salvation Army.' In like manner she thanks the E Plus workers. Upon her departure she hears, 'Because you have given and done what you could, I will pour out my blessing on you. You can never out give me.'

Episode 4. Another soldier hears God's voice and, blessed with the gift of helps, he reaches the store and offers a small portion of his valuable time to sort books. The manager is amazed and wonders what is going on. As the man returns to the corps he feels the joy of the Lord.

Episode 5. Once again a soldier leaves the scene, goes home and she does what she does best. Armed with her baking she thanks the staff at the store and E Plus in the only way that she knows how, and returns to the meeting with a fuller heart than when she left singing, 'How wondrous, God gives to those who give, running out and flowing over'.

Episode 6. Another soldier sees the glimmer of a tear fall, and compassionately seeks out the Salvo store volunteer who just sat and watched as his mother died. There is nothing to offer but an understanding and open heart. But this is graciously received. The worshipper departs, promising to return soon, his heart filled with love.

Episode 7. The corps officer, inspired by his godly corps, visits a group of staff and volunteers whom God has been preparing, and finds fallow ground––a people ready to receive the planting of seed. They understand 'love' because they have experienced it through his soldiers. They want to get downstream in this river of God's grace. The CO returns 'carrying in the sheaves', knowing the miracles that occur when tiny seeds––or small acts of kindness––are sown. In the season of need God uses them and through them, produce the treasure of life––eternal life.

Word of God's power to multiply the smallest of gifts and sacrifice spread through other Corps where they had been praying for showers, and the call went out: 'Seed the clouds of doubt and discouragement with tiny particles that feel like the dust of earthly striving'. Give what you have and God will take your sacrifice and perform his miracle. Do what you can do and you will be a witness to how God can bring a flood, but he wants your small dust of––giving away of your acts or talents.

Brainstorm

- » For us to become 'a people of praise', what are the costs and what are the benefits?

- » When we receive, do we recognise grace––the gift we did not deserve or earn, but the provision that we need?

- » Do we believe in self-sufficiency? How do we learn to meditate on its opposite (or balancer)?

- » What can we do to encourage their growth and maturity of grace and gifts in an environment that otherwise hinders normal growth?

- » How can we begin to change a culture of 'I need, I want' to 'I have been blessed'? If we do change the culture, how much will we need the belief 'God gives the increase'?

- » Do we believe that if we have the right attitude, the right acts will follow?
- » If we believe that God supplies our every need, why do we emotionally and financially feel needy?

One Day...

Vision 12 – Salvos Stores / Trade = Fair Trade

'… that Salvo Stores and the trade department become responsible outlets for Fair Trade goods.'

Jean Roper

Fair Trade is a social movement that promotes the idea that fair payment should be made to those in developing countries who produce goods such as coffee, cocoa, tea, honey and handicrafts. This in turn has a positive effect on social and environmental standards in these areas. While the movement has been around since the 1940s, it's only been in recent years that a formal definition of Fair Trade has been established, and international organisations have been created to link producers, retailers and exporters.

So why should The Salvation Army be concerned about Fair Trade? If we take our mission statement seriously—that we are raised up by God to transform lives and reform society—then how can we not take an interest in being responsible retailers and responsible consumers? We live in a consumerist, materialistic society. It's hard not to be caught up with all the comfort and pleasure that our lifestyles bring. But we do have a choice in the way we spend our money. And as an organisation we have a choice in what we choose to support.

So what can we do about it? We can think about this in two ways: how can we act as individuals, and how can we, as The Salvation Army, be responsible retailers through Salvo Stores and Salvation Army Supplies (trade department)?

Firstly, as an organisation we can act in the following ways:

- In our Salvo stores and in the trade department, we can endeavour to sell Fair Trade products. For example, the trade department could tell their suppliers that they will only stock products that are made in Australia or other economically sound countries.
- Become a member of the Fair Trade Association of Australia and New Zealand. This will enable us to be in contact with other Fair Trade suppliers and increase the amount of fair trade products we stock.
- Our website could have a link to an online shopping area that sells Fair Trade products such as handicrafts, tea and coffee.
- Introduce Sally Ann items to our product line. These items, such as handicrafts and knitwear, are made by the disenfranchised in Bangladesh and sold to provide profit directly to the individuals who make them. Similarly, we could stock items that are made here in Australia.

A dream worth living for the Australia Southern Territory **79**

» At THQ and DHQs we could actively use only Fair Trade coffee in our lunchrooms and canteens. Even at a corps level this would be easy to implement.
» Act as an advocate on behalf of the Fair Trade movement. More and more individuals are aware of fair trade products and we need to show that we are an active voice and an active player. Previously, the trade department has existed only to serve the needs of Salvationists. It's time to acknowledge that we also need to be ethically responsible traders.

As individuals, we can also play an active part:

» We can access resources about Fair Trade, sign online petitions, and receive newsletters.
» We can demands Fair Trade products in our local cafes, restaurants and even supermarkets.
» We can do our own research before we buy products and make responsible and informed choices.

Brainstorm

Check out the following websites for more information:

justsalvos.com
(Australia Southern Territory Social Justice website)

www.salvationist.org
(search for Sally Ann International Fair Trade Project)

www.fta.org.au
(Fair Trade Association of Australia and New Zealand)

www.ifat.org
(International Fair Trade Association)

www.fairtrade.asn.au
(People for Fair Trade—Australia)

www.oxfam.org.au
(Oxfam Australia)

www.globalconduct.com.au
(Global Conduct)

Vision 13 – Commercial Fair Trade

'…that our commercial department at THQ become a resource and focal point for facilitating our increasing efforts in Fair Trade.'

Lieutenant Sonia Jeffrey

I love this part of the Dream. It stirs me. It should stir us each. To think our Salvation Army could use its existing resources to engage in justice-based trading which impacts positively on developing nations astounds me. But it shouldn't. We were born for this practical brand of mission.

The Fair Trade concept is not new to The Salvation Army. Etched into the pages of our history are examples of the spirit of Fair Trade—fair work, fair wages for all. It's a call for justice on many levels.

It calls for workers to be redeemed, for products to be safe and of exceedingly good quality and for profits to return to honour the toil of the worker. Furthermore, the Fair Trade ethos invites us to partner—through our buying of particular products—to enhance the lives of communities around the globe.

The local Fair Trade story was as close as Westwood Place in Melbourne's heart. The Salvation Army's Hamodova Tea

Company, in 1897, brewed quality tea leaves that ensured a fair deal for Sri Lankan missionaries.

Booth's famous 'Match Factory' campaign produced safe matches with Fair Trade ethics printed across every box. His vision to employ people in ways that would add—not subtract—value to their lives was a legacy we can live out today.

We should not be surprised then, that in 2007 the leaders of this territory have endorsed the Fair Trade principle, ensuring all corps and centres should promote and sanction fair trade products.

This decision calls all Salvationists to think seriously about the products that are purchased and distributed on behalf of The Salvation Army. Furthermore, it challenges all soldiers to think about what kind of products they buy for their own homes.

Every product we consume has a story—some more gruesome than others. Two of the staples of western culture, coffee and chocolate, have been scrutinised in recent years, as the story of their production involves slavery and deception.

The Salvation Army has a God-given window of opportunity to change the lives of small communities that produce the products we daily enjoy. Through our well-organised administrative systems and partnership between many of our THQ departments, it is possible for us to take a lead on the dissemination of Fair Trade products.

We envisage every corps serving Fair Trade tea and coffee in every kitchen, at every home league and in the waiting areas of every welfare service.

We dream for every centre to offer Fair Trade products to every client, enabling us to share the justice dream with them as we offer counsel and care.

We see our commercial department sourcing deals with suppliers that ensure that justice is done not only in our financial dealings, but also in the manner it serves the territory.

The Fair Trade dream cannot come true overnight. It requires Salvationists like you and me to ask God to break our hearts for communities who labour under unjust conditions for our gain. It will require us to ask tougher questions, to do more research when engaging companies to provide us with goods and services.

It will demand from us each a mindset that asks not what's in this for me, but what can be restored to those whose lives have been lessened by exploitative commercial pursuits.

We can do this! The Salvation Army is beautifully positioned to pick up the fair trade baton that was handed to us in our infancy. Soldiers, officers, friends—will you join us?

Brainstorm:

What corps can do:
- Get a start up kit from justsalvos.com
- Ask small groups to research communities that have benefited from Fair Trade.
- Share their stories in public meetings.
- Sell Fair Trade chocolate, tea, sugar and cocoa in Salvos stores, at corps fairs and corps-based cafes.
- Host 'Fair Trade tasting nights' so people can taste and choose the products the corps wish to serve.

What corps officers can do:
- With your leadership teams, review every product and service the corps purchases. Ask if the companies are reputable, if they treat their staff with dignity and whether they are maintaining corporate social responsibility.
- Advise your DHQ and THQ of your findings, helping them source more just deals for services purchased on behalf of the territory.

What soldiers can do:
- Switch to Fair Trade tea, coffee, cocoa, chocolate and sugar in your homes.

- Ask your local stores to stock fair trade products—specify which ones.
- Download the Fair Trade guides from the Stop the Traffik international website.
- Do some internet research into coffee and chocolate producing communities.
- Write to members of parliament to raise the Fair Trade issues, particularly as they relate to Australian-produced coffee and chocolate products.

Vision 14 — Tracing the lost

'…that the Family Tracing Service be expanded to find those souls who have been lost to the Army, assisting in bringing them home, where they belong.'

Pam Warr

In the musical 1776 there is a poignant moment when George Washington asks 'Is anybody there? Is anybody listening? Does anybody care?'.

I am sure that our Founder, William Booth, heard similar words when he answered God's call to bring into being The Salvation Army, founded in a time of industrial revolution in England.

Did you know…that because of the tragic working conditions in phosphorous match factories in the 1800s, many labourers developed 'phossy jaw'? Exposure to white phosphorous led to the deadly condition where the jaw is eaten away.

William Booth could not stand by and let this continue so he set in motion the development of the safety match we know today.

One Day...

He had a dream and did something about it!

Did you know…that in the affluent London society of the same era, advertisements in daily papers appealed for young girls to work in stately homes as pantry maids and scullery maids?

These girls left home and often never reached their destination, becoming easy prey to the procurers of the day. William Booth began to receive letters from parents asking if The Salvation Army could trace their missing daughters.

In July 1885, William Booth published a letter in *The War Cry* stating that The Salvation Army would offer assistance to any anxious parents. In October that year the first *War Cry* insert for a missing person was published.

William Booth had a dream and the Family Tracing Service has now been in operation for more than 120 years!

Did you know…that The Salvation Army Family Tracing Service has offices in every country in which the Army flag flies?

I have a dream that The Salvation Army could look for 'lost friends and comrades'—people who were once connected with our corps—and make contact in an attempt to heal past hurts and win them back to the Master.

Can you imagine an Army mobilised, deploying modern technology to make these searches possible and making contact with those who walked through our doors in days gone by?

Can you imagine linking up with corps cadets that you have not seen for some 25 years or more?

Can you imagine finding some former songster or bandsman you sat next to many years ago?

Can you imagine the wonderful celebrations that would take place if our former beloved soldiers and comrades came to sit with us again in our citadels?

Can you imagine the joy in heaven over one lost prodigal coming back to the Master?

Can you imagine that this is all possible, but not without a great deal of prayer and God-given wisdom?

Two sisters came to the Family Tracing Service looking for a brother they hadn't seen for more than 50 years. He was last

heard of in the UK, so we forwarded the enquiry to London, but not before the two sisters and I spent time in prayer asking our Heavenly Father to guide those in London in their search.
A week later, one of the enquirers received a telephone call from their brother. He had longed to make contact but had had difficulty tracing his sisters who were both married. When I met the sisters again, they said 'your prayers have been answered'.

We have brothers and sisters in Christ and the bond we share is no less. My dream cannot come to fruition without a lot of teamwork and, above all, prayer.

'Except I am moved with compassion, how dwelleth thy Spirit in me.'

Brainstorm

» Form a group of comrades who will set time aside each day for prayer as the dream unfolds.

» Search through corps rolls to ascertain names of those lost to the corps. YP rolls may hold great potential.

» Search electoral rolls and telephone books and internet sites when a list of names has been gathered.

» After locating people from the list, invite them to a meal in your home and encourage them to feel welcome and attend a holiness/salvation meeting.

» Arrange a 'Back To' social event when a number have been traced and visited.

One Day...

Vision 15 – Adding to our number daily

'…that we would never have another day in our existence where someone was not brought to Christ.'

Bram Southwell

[For the purpose of this chapter, I have rephrased the above to '…that there would never be another day of no rejoicing'.]

Jesus supported the idea that there is a great party held in heaven over the repentance of one sinner (Luke 15:7). He emphasised again and again the inclusive nature of the kingdom of God—everyone is welcome.

Salvationists know this joy too. There is delight when we know of a wanderer's return. We love to celebrate, even though our response may be trifling compared to what goes on among those heavenly witnesses. If this dream is to be realised, the party becomes the mother of all enduring celebrations.

But aren't we running ahead of ourselves here? This dream is really a dream for effective, productive outreach. Undoubtedly, saving souls is the foundational mission objective of The Salvation Army. The dream, as it is interpreted and applied at the level of the individual Salvationist, becomes a personal, purposeful and proactive assignment.

A much-quoted verse is 'Carry each other's burdens, and…fulfil the law of Christ' (Galatians 6: 2). In order to do this, I must first be acquainted with the burden. Our understanding of a person is directly proportional to our willingness to listen to them. We need to be prepared to spend time doing this. This becomes a priority and, inevitably, it will be ranked alongside all the other duties and concerns in our life. Just how available are we going to be? Are we going to let this happen? The choice is ours.

Mother Theresa shared profound wisdom when she referred to her own life as being 'like a little pencil in the hand of God.' Having lived in India before the introduction of the ubiquitous Biro pen, I have seen the way a little pencil progressively becomes an even smaller pencil in the hand of the user—until it is literally worn away. Devotion to God through selfless service to others will wear us away too.

Now let's address the issue of the mission field of the family. If ever the Great Commission (Matthew 25:31–46) is relevant, it is within the home of the Christian. For it's in the home that we can see others hungry, thirsty, sick and/or naked. Sadly too, we sometimes see those who are strangers or in prison.

I have a dream—that every Salvationist's home will be a safe house for those who live there.

There are some serious statistics in The Scandal of the Evangelical Conscience by Ron J. Sider (Baker Books 2005). The picture is not a pretty one. Sider refers to a 'crisis of disobedience' in the evangelical world today in respect to marriage and family life. The evils of workaholic behaviour, financial irresponsibility, inappropriate use of leisure, TV and internet addiction diminish the ability of parents to nurture children and bring them to Christ.

Parents need vision and strategies to manage family life wisely. Many do it well. Some struggle. For others, it is a disaster zone. Perhaps the worst heartrending words that express the regret of parents and children are, 'If only…'.

This is not God's plan. It is not his kingdom. I propose that the mission field of the family stands equal with all other fields.

God's plan is that families are blessed. With Paul we can say of spouses and children 'You are our glory and joy' (1 Thessalonians 2:19—20). But it is double joy, because heaven is celebrating too. The mission has been accomplished.

Brainstorm

General

- » It is relatively easy to define a mission objective (dream), but not always as easy to implement a plan and measure the outcome. Comment.
- » Is it enough to practice lifestyle evangelism?
- » Are there further steps required to bring a person to Christ?
- » How does your corps provide help to dysfunctional families in your community?
- » What strategies could be put in place to strengthen family life?
- » How would you rate the children's ministry of your corps?

Personal

- » How are relationships within your family?
- » Are there people in your life for whom 'extra' grace is required in your relationship with them?
- » How are disagreements handled in your family?
- » How are negative emotions (fear, anger, disappointment, depression) handled?
- » What prison doors may need to be opened?
    a. Guilt over past failure
    b. Acquisitiveness and financial irresponsibility

c. Time management issues
  d. Alienation
  e. Insecurity
  f. Addictive behaviour
  g. Health issues
» 'Yes, I carry other's burdens, but I find that they are very heavy'. Are there answers to this?
» Are there other measures, not raised by the writer, which should be considered?
» How can I take hope from the theme?
» What can I do?

References:
Ron Sider, in *The Scandal of the Evangelical Conscience* (Baker Books, 2005) writes, 'Born again Christians divorce at about the same rate as everyone else. Self-centred materialism is seducing evangelicals and rapidly destroying our earlier, slightly more generous giving. Only six percent of born-again Christians tithe. Born-again Christians justify and engage in sexual promiscuity (both pre-marital sex and adultery) at astonishing rates. Racism and perhaps physical abuse of wives seem to be worse in evangelical circles than elsewhere. This is scandalous behaviour for people who claim to be born-again by the Holy Spirit and to enjoy the presence of the Risen Lord in their lives.' (p. 28).

One Day...

Vision 16 – Growing Army

'…that our soldiers roll would only be an increasing reality as would our worship and discipleship meetings.'

Commissioner Doug Davis

This aspect of the dream brings together the enfolding and the feeding work of a corps for the benefit of the flock entrusted to its care. It is also the personal mission of Salvationists. Soul saving and soldier making is an essential, shared objective.

Each Salvationist is 'an individual agent of the Lord Jesus Christ and has to show personal enterprise in the endeavours to win people one by one'[1]. Further, 'the corps is the basic unit of the evangelistic purpose of the Army… Its main task is to lead people to a saving knowledge of Jesus Christ'[2].

The twofold aspect of the dream involves hands and feet—Salvationists mobilised to win others for the Lord—and also the commitment of hearts and minds to provide quality worship and discipling experiences for our people. These twin dimensions are inseparable.

---

1 *Chosen to be a Soldier*, Chapter XI, Sect. 2, para.3
2 *Chosen to be a Soldier*, Chapter X, Sect. 3, para.1

Hands and feet:

General Paul Rader suggests that William Booth's reluctance to use the word 'church' for his embryonic Salvation Army was because 19th century British churches were ingrown and self absorbed. 'In terms of mission they had lost the scent and were in danger of missing the quarry. Having shut themselves safely into holy enclaves, which had forgotten to say, "Come!" and were often not too eager to "Go!"…'[1].

Over time there have been subtle changes in Salvation Army vocabulary. Do the changes indicate that the Founder's assessment of the churches of his time could now apply to some corps? A timeline could be drawn using the following terms and graphed against souls saved and soldiers made at each transition in this chain: warfare » service » mission » ministry.

Soldiers rolls will not increase due to some mystical spiritual osmosis won from heaven by the desperate hopes and prayers of the faithful. To ensure effective mission in our corps, it is essential that both group and personal evangelism activities are given priority. The hands and feet aspect of this imperative should be modelled by our corps officers and shared with those soldiers who are motivated and equipped to serve as soul winners.

---

1   *Word & Deed*, Vol. 1, No. 1, November 1998

Quite a challenge! But certainly not impossible if bathed in prayer and pursued with Holy Spirit daring.

Hearts and minds:
Our worship and discipleship meetings require the service of hearts and minds. 'I will pray with my spirit, but I will also pray with my mind; I will sing with my spirit, but I will also sing with my mind,' says Paul (1 Corinthians 14:15, NIV). Meetings planned with passion and purpose will motivate soldiery to march out of the hall to fight well for the Captain of their Salvation. What is sung, said and done in meetings should be intentional, intelligent and inspired, giving the Holy Spirit adequate elbow room along the way.

Many corps meetings have become largely the work of the officers to the exclusion of soldiers. This negates the priesthood of believers—our heritage as children of the reformation and members of an evangelistic movement. Opportunities for public prayer and testimony will breathe new vitality into corps meetings that have drifted into a leader focused format. Let's recover the kind of meeting characterised by song 608 *The Song Book of The Salvation Army*, verse 3:

> Souls shall be truly converted to thee,
> From all the bondage of Satan be free,
> Made into soldiers to fight well for thee,
> Lord, we believe; Lord, we believe.

Brainstorm

» Is your corps indifferent to the importance of outreach? If so, why? Has evangelism been made too demanding and difficult? Is witnessing a more comfortable idea? If so, share experiences of witnessing.

» How often does your senior pastoral care council (census board) hold meetings? Are the corps rolls then thoroughly reviewed and absentees prayed for and followed up?

» Check the corps address list to ascertain if it contains prospective adherents and soldiers. Arrange for a suitable person to speak privately with those identified.

» Plan and organise an interest meeting with afternoon tea for the above people.

» Ask your corps council to devise and photocopy a simple invitation to corps activities. Place it in letterboxes in your street along with copies of *Warcry*. After three weeks of deliveries, go and knock on some doors—but only after a prayer meeting at the corps has prepared the way.

- » Hand out flyers in the main shopping street inviting people to corps activities.

- » Ask the corps officer to arrange for a photograph and article in the local newspaper featuring a corps youngster with an elderly person who attends the corps. Provide the corps flag as a backdrop and include a copy of the soldiers' covenant as a focal point.

- » Hold a soldiership renewal Sunday meeting including prepared testimonies from the oldest and newest soldiers and adherents.

- » Display a locally prepared promotional notice for soldiership in the corps foyer. Announce a soldiership preparation seminar.

- » Hold a discussion group after a Sunday meeting during coffee time to explore ways of involving attendees in worship participation.

Vision 17 – Pervasive proliferation

> *'…that the proliferation of new ministry openings would be so common and normal that we would have to appoint personnel just to keep track of it, most often after the fact.'*
>
> *General Eva Burrows (Rtd)*

It will be great when that dream becomes a reality. Can you visualise it? Exciting, isn't it! New ministries springing up everywhere. Fantastic new expressions of mission bringing us into contact with new people, and helping those people find a new lifestyle in Christ through the gospel.

Everyone wants to belong to something that is alive and growing; not something that's just maintaining the status quo. How is your corps doing?

The key thought, the key phrase, in Commissioner Knaggs' expressed dream is 'new ministry openings'. Ministries reaching into the community to make and build new relationships must be relevant. So how do such ministries arise?

Spontaneously really, when members of a corps have their finger on the pulse of the felt needs and interests of the community;

when corps folk have a passion to interact with people and bring them alive with the truths of the gospel. For example, observe the success of the new ministry Mainly Music which meets the need of mothers and preschool children. It also establishes warm relationships with the mums so they find friendship and get to know people who can offer them help and counsel when needed.

There are plenty of opportunities out there. Look for those opportunities. Discover the concerns of people in your community. What ministry programs could you introduce in your area? What resources are there in your community to set you off?

I know of a corps that was approached by the police to see if they could do something— anything—about the kids who were hanging out in the shopping mall and behaving in a very disruptive manner. Corps folk arranged a barbecue and a bright program of activities that led to relationships with young people who had a lot of needs. A breakfast before school was organised; this led to a youth group on Friday nights, and to counselling on drugs and a meaningful engagement with the young people, many of whom became turned on to Jesus Christ.

For whom might a corps initiate new ministries in your community?

Young families? Exciting programs for the whole family to be together, with fun and happy times—providing opportunities to make valuable contacts.

Health issues? Both men and women are keenly interested in health these days. I heard of a corps where it was discovered that there was concern among some women about menopause, and the offering of a course on this subject led to the formation of a women's fellowship.

A club or group for single parents and unmarried singles? There are increasing numbers in every community, and many are looking for support—socially, emotionally and spiritually.

Unemployed people? Many do want to work, and would appreciate opportunities to do volunteering. This provides for further ministries.

Environmental issues? People are passionate about this and have it high on their agenda. Offer your council a clean-up day or some other activity you discover people want to get involved in.

How can you discover resources in your community that will give you openings and new opportunities for mission and ministry?
» Local newspapers, both as a source and a resource.

- » Contact schools and principals who are often very keen to accept help.
- » Get in touch with local police, who have a good knowledge of the needs of the community. They are right in the front line of the community.
- » Local councils and councillors who can tell you where the gaps are, and where needs are not being met.
- » Read books by people such as Hugh Mackay who understand and highlight the needs of Australian communities today.

How exciting it would be if corps launched out to needy groups, and divisional headquarters had a big surprise when they found out about these new ministries afterwards. Commissioner Knaggs is dreaming of a day when this will be occurring naturally everywhere throughout the territory, introducing new people to the corps, and introducing new people to Jesus Christ. Corps with an evangelistic culture like this inspired by the Holy Spirit will be abuzz with excitement as every believer becomes fully engaged in helping friends and family, neighbours and strangers encounter Jesus.

Brainstorm

- Identify the people in your corps who are passionate about forming relationships with others in the community and sharing Christ.
- Can they form a group of soldiers and officers who, under the inspiration of the Holy Spirit, come up with startling new ideas? The Holy Spirit is an innovator; he never does things in the same old way.
- Who knows the needs of your community?
- How can you make positive contacts with the various agencies in the community who can lead you to the lonely, the isolated, the distressed?
- What are the needs of young people in your community?
- What volunteering opportunities can you offer?
- Do the soldiers of the corps know how to share their faith with someone else? To have a meaningful face-to-face encounter? Or are they too scared? Too timid? Don't know how? You can find out. Find the right teacher to lead a course to equip them in faith-sharing.

One Day...

Vision 18 – Creative ministry

'…that those gifted with creative ministry gifts would have every opportunity to employ these very skills in the work of the Army.'

Major David Mundy

If we believe that Christ died for all, then there must be a place for all in the kingdom of God. We enter that kingdom with our skills, hobbies, interests and more, ready to discover that special place where God would have us be.

Those with a creative ministry are called upon to occupy that place and take on an awesome responsibility, to imitate God in that unique way—to imitate the Creator. Just as God has been and continues to be varied in his creation, so those who have this creative ministry are varied in style too.

It's easy to make use of a musician or vocalist in The Salvation Army, but what of the poet or painter, wood turner or cook, dancer or computer graphics expert? What of the gardener or florist, the quilter or welder? They are all found in the kingdom and they each can contribute beautifully in worship as well as in other avenues within the Army.

Seek out such people. Urge them to contribute to the life of the Army, encourage their experimentation in creativity, and don't be surprised when God speaks to you through their creative expression.

We live in a creative and stimulating world. Communication styles have developed to incredible levels. A Commissioner has a dream and I have a copy of it soon afterwards. In my life, I have gone from wireless and slide projectors to multimedia and MP3s.

In the kingdom of God there are those who have skills in these new levels of communication and creative fields—people of varying ages who can express their creative skills in the worship environment. Let them.

I have been impressed with the 24/7 prayer reports. Throughout the territory, creativity has been used in prayer. There have been different displays, varying environments, differing prose styles. The ideas have been shared, and probably copied, developed, and stimulated others. What better compliment than for someone to copy your idea. Creative minds are out there. Find them.

I enjoy sensory worship, using all five senses in worship. When was the last time you used your nose when worshipping God?

The other month I was invited to contribute to worship. I had been developing a prayer picnic concept. In a garden setting, a low table was set with food that is mentioned in the Bible, food with symbolic significance. Music played, the birds sang. Those gathered read of the symbolism on a leaflet, then came and ate, choosing the food carefully, digesting the symbolism. We saw, we heard, we smelled the aromas, we felt, we tasted. Such an idea had been created in my mind. I waited for the right occasion, and I was soon asked.

If other creative people are like me then they, too, will need to be asked. Some of us are not too good at volunteering. Ask us.

Creative people think outside the square. A creative person will not only see the wood turner and think of the amount of money that could be raised on a street stall. A creative person will see the skill and use it in worship as an example of how beauty can come after much hardship. A creative person will see a stand for a floral arrangement. A creative person will visualise wooden pens that could be given to new soldiers when they sign their covenants. A creative person can…

Now I look at those touch screens at the shopping centres.
Imagine having one of those in the prayer room.
I, too, dream.

Brainstorm

» List those people you know who have a creative streak. List their creative style/s.
» How can such creativity contribute to the worship and other aspects of life within the local Salvation Army?
» What creative ministry could be used to stimulate/involve each of the five senses in sensory worship?
» Conduct a review of the facilities at your local Salvation Army. For example:
   a. Consider what a new person might experience (using all five senses)
   b. What is the main entrance like?
   c. What is the focal point of the worship area?
   d. Is the atmosphere of the building cheerful? Depressing? Cluttered?
   e. What does the notice board look like?
   f. Sit in another seat in the worship area. What differences do you see?
   g. Is the building child friendly? Is it accessible to wheelchairs?
   h. Return to your list of creative people. Approach them for ideas to improve the local facilities.

Vision 19 – Creative worship

'…that our worship would be filled with creative means to celebrate God's provisions and presence among us.'

Brian Hogg

'The Salvation Army wants reality and not ritualism in our worship. Our constant aim is to avoid becoming merely an audience that does not participate. We want a congregation where all in spirit and truth are one in worship. Our emphasis has always been on personal participation.'

– *General Wilfred Kitching 1963*

There can be little argument that our God is a creative God. What we create with our own hands, ability and skill can inspire us and help us to contemplate God's own creation. Clever, really! God allows us to use the creative talents he has placed in us to give us an insight into his own creative genius.

The pinnacle of God's creative genius was for him to conceive, design and implement our own salvation through his son.

When we come together in a collective worship experience, we celebrate God's genius in providing for us this means of salvation.

We marvel at his creative power throughout the world and in the lives of his people as we dwell in his presence. David's prayer is an instant reminder of the creative power of our God: 'Create in me a clean heart, O God; and renew a right spirit within me,' (Psalm 51:10).

Who else can create a clean heart but the God of creation himself? Our true worship comes from our heart. How we express the feelings of our heart is as varied as the creative talents we, as God's church, possess. Since God created us, he knows we need a multitude of creative expressions to help us bring his people into his presence and the knowledge of his love for them.

Duke Ellington once said, 'I believe that no matter what the skill of a drummer or saxophonist, if this is the thing that he does best, and he offers it sincerely from the heart (or as an accompaniment to) his worship, then it will not be unacceptable because of the instrument, be it pipe or tom-tom. If a man is troubled, he moans and cries when he worships, when a man feels that that which he enjoys in this life is only because of the grace of God, he rejoices, he sings, and sometimes dances (and so it was with David)'.

I sometimes appreciate this quote more when I'm at the cricket one-day finals at the MCG. There in my work clothes, I'm surrounded by those dressed in various green and gold garments with their faces painted; some men (with their shirts off) have their favourite player's name emblazoned on their chests. Some simply quietly clap, while others scream and shout.

What a celebration! What expression and emotion! That's when it hits me. While I mightn't support the cricketers in the same way others do, I'm pleased that we are all cheering on the same side. Imagine what our collective worship experience could be like if we were prepared to involve a wide variety of expression and accept it for what it is.

Contemporary worship is about engaging and connecting with the individuals in the congregation. We each have our own way of learning and absorbing information. So it helps to convey information in different ways. What an opportunity for us to utilise the creative tapestry God has given his church to display his creative and re-creative power.

> '"Tradition! Tradition!" you say. No! Innovation, initiative, creativity, adaptability, ingenuity, flexibility, all harnessed to these timeless principles'
>
> *- William Booth*

One Day...

Brainstorm

» With your Bible study group or section take a quick poll:
   a. How many people listen to talkback radio?
   b. How many prefer 50s rock and roll?
   c. Who is the favourite musical group and/or soloist?

(There will likely be a good variety of answers. Why do we generally only provide one style of music in church?)

You can take a similar poll for films and movie styles and discuss the ways in which we differ in our likes/dislikes.

» Discuss the merit/value of using non-musical elements in worship.

Responsive/collective scripture reading:
   a. The Word is valuable. Do we use it enough in our services?
   b. How many different ways can we open-the-Word with our congregation?

Responsive/collective prayer:
   a. Do we use prayer in ways that involve and engage our people?
   b. Do we truly model the value of prayer in our services?

The use of video:
   a. How does the use of a popular film bring insight into the Christian life?
   b. Can popular culture have anything to say about faith and God?

The use of drama:
   a. Can drama create different responses to a given situation?
   b. Can live drama help us to engage with the feelings of others? How?

Using symbolic, tactile imagery:
   a. Using an object to meditate/contemplate can be a powerful reminder of God's presence, grace and mercy. Describe an object that you have that means something special to you.

Visual stimuli:
   a. What value do you see in decorating your meeting space differently?
   b. How could you use visual props to bring a focus to a particular meeting?
   c. Compile a list of creative activities that your congregation is involved in (this could include photography, painting, banner making, quilting, dance, drama, various styles of music, woodwork, metalwork, patchwork, needle craft,

scrapbooking, sculpture and creative installations, model making, pottery, script writing, poetry, etc,).

d. Discuss and create ways in which these creative expressions can be brought into the collective worship experience.
e. Hold a special meeting where items created by your congregation are displayed.
f. Use the opportunity to focus attention on God's creative genius.
g. Create opportunities for different art forms to be used together.

# Vision 20 – 24/7 prayer

'…that our 24/7 Prayer Initiatives will be adopted by individual corps throughout the territory all the time.'

Captain Robert Evans

'Call to me and I will answer you and tell you great and unsearchable things you do not know'

– Jeremiah 33:3

When God revealed this prophetic word to me on 9 September 2005 at Noarlunga, I never imagined the extraordinary impact it would have on my understanding and expectation of prayer. What I did know was that God had been calling me for a long time to do something significant regarding prayer—only I had no idea what that was to look like.

This call first came when I was at Palmerston (NT). I was given the Transformations video and was inspired by God's prophetic call for churches to unite together in prayer, resulting in miraculous community transformations in a number of cities around the world.

This inspiration grew into a passion to bring churches together to pray in our community and was further fuelled while stationed at

Horsham (Vic.) where I saw Transformations 2. We engaged the corps for the first time in a 24-hour prayer meeting where God's call became stronger, but not yet clearer. All I knew was the churches needed to unite in prayer.

The flame that was burning within my spirit received a tremendous boost when I read a powerful booklet called The Prayer of Obedience. It was at this time God spoke to me from Jeremiah 33:3 and I knew any transformation had to begin with my own prayer life. During the following months we hosted a couple of 24-hour prayer events and I felt a clear prophetic call to open a prayer room in Noarlunga.

I didn't know about the existence of the international 24/7 prayer movement until I met Captain Stephen Court, who was a guest speaker at the Adelaide One Mission Conference. I learned about the 'War Room' in Vancouver and was introduced to the book *Red Moon Rising*, which exposed me to the beginnings and inspiration of 24/7 prayer.

This book, and my encounter with Stephen, gave clarity to what had been brewing in my spirit for several years. God wanted a 24/7 prayer room in our city. I shared this vision with some other Christians who attended a combined church prayer meeting at our corps. Following the meeting a working group of awesome prayer warriors who embraced this exciting vision was formed.

During the past 18 months, we have worked towards the establishment of the prayer room and, despite barriers, busyness and bureaucracy, God would not release me from this calling. At the beginning of August 2007, our corps signed up for the territorial year of prayer and it seemed right to use our rostered week of prayer as a launch for our combined churches 24/7 prayer room. We ran the prayer room from our corps for the first seven weeks before moving into a shop front in Huntfield Heights.

At the same time God spoke to me from Jeremiah 33:3, he also gave me a prophesy for our corps from Jeremiah 33:6–9 which has formed the foundation of our corps vision. What is exciting about this vision is that we have absolutely no hope of achieving it! Only God can bring health and healing, only God can bring peace and security, only God can bring freedom and unity, only God can forgive and restore!

'Then…all nations on earth that hear of all the good things I do for it will be in awe and will tremble at the abundant prosperity and peace I provide for it' (Jeremiah 33:9). We are totally dependent on God to fulfil his vision, making this 24/7 prayer room fundamental to our mission strategy as a corps.

For too long The Salvation Army has become known for what we do. I believe it is time for our renown to come from what Christ has done and is continuing to do. We are on the threshold of a significant outpouring of God's Spirit. I believe for The Salvation Army to become an Acts 2 church, we need to become Acts 1 people who are 'joined together constantly in prayer'.

I am excited to see God at work and stand in awe at what he is doing at this time. I am convinced that the best is yet to come and claim the promise God gave through Joshua: 'Consecrate yourselves, for tomorrow the Lord will do amazing things among you' (Joshua 3:5).

Brainstorm

Websites
- Visit the international 24/7 Prayer website to learn more about 24/7 prayer and see what God is currently doing in prayer rooms around the world. This site also has some very helpful resources and online assistance to help you set up a prayer room (short or long term): www.24-7prayer.com
- Visit The Salvation Army Australia Southern Territory 24/7 webpage to find out how your corps can get involved in the territorial year of prayer: www.salvationarmy.org.au/24-7
- Visit the Onkaparinga combined churches 24/7 prayer room website to find out more about how the Noarlunga Corps is involved in 24/7 prayer in our local community:
- www.24-7prayeronkaparinga.com

Resources
These books have inspired me in my own prayer journey and the establishment of a 24/7 prayer room:
- *The Prayer of Obedience*, Dr. Stuart Robinson, City Harvest Publications, 2005
- *Red Moon Rising—The Story of 24-7 Prayer*, Pete Greig & Dave Roberts, Kingsway Publications, 2005
- *Prayer—Does It Make Any Difference?*, Philip Yancey, Hodder & Stoughton, 2006

- » The 24-7 Prayer Manual (with CD Rom), order online through www.24-7prayer.com
- » (From the 24-7prayer.com: '…the definitive "How To Run a Prayer Room for Dummies". It covers everything from how to motivate your group to creative ideas for building an inspirational prayer space. The wisdom and advice in these pages could save you a lot of work, learn from our mistakes and make your prayer room rock.')
- » The Transformations documentary series is a must-see for anyone wanting evidence of what can happen when churches unite together in prayer:
- » Transformations 1 & 2 (video/DVD), produced by the Sentinel Group, hosted by George Otis Jr.

Scripture
- » Jeremiah 33:3, 6–9
- » Acts 1:14, 2:42–47
- » 2 Chronicles 7:14
- » Joshua 3:5
- » Isaiah 51:1–3, 62:6–7
- » John 15:1–8
- » Zechariah 3:1–10

Vision 21 – Lighthouses of prayer

***'…that we would establish Lighthouses of Prayer to
cover our neighbourhoods with grace.'***

Kirsten Gourd

In Acts 13:47, Luke quotes the prophet Isaiah, 'For this is what the Lord has commanded us; "I have made you a light for the Gentiles, that you may bring salvation to the ends of the earth."'

As an aid for aerial and maritime navigation, a lighthouse shines great beams of light over the darkest seas and into the darkest night sky to guide boats safely into harbour and aeroplanes safely to land. In the same way, as an institution of God's powerful kindness and grace, a church is not merely called, but commanded to shine great beams of God's presence and love, bring salvation to our communities, and then to the world.

A church is truly doing its job if it is serving as a lighthouse. Notice a lighthouse doesn't point its light inwardly so it can enjoy all the warmth, comfort and safety it wants. Similarly, the lighthouse of the church doesn't shine on Christians alone. It puts most of its energy and power into shining outwardly, to the unsaved, lighting up the darkness that surrounds it. In the same way, in making up the church, each of us are called by Christ to 'let our light shine before men' (Matthew 6:16a) and to give light to the darkness around us.

Your corps is probably already a lighthouse, giving light to its surrounding community. It just needs a little tweaking to become a lighthouse of prayer.

Corps are busy places and prayer must be intentional. It is easy to only shine inwardly and pray individually for what directly concerns us. However, the gold is in the labour of intercession, in the praying with, and for, others. It is this act of shining outwardly, the laying on of hands, joining with one another in agonising and unrelenting prayer that is part of the mission of the church—a part that is easily forgotten in the business of church life.

To shine outwardly, you need a source of power. If prayer is communicating with the ultimate power source—our Heavenly Father—then prayer should be an integral part of your corps. If it isn't, then I suggest some alterations need to be made.

The Salvation Army does a stellar job of welcoming in the sick, the needy, the broken, addicted and poor. However, what do we do once they're in? Feed them and send them on their merry way?

Feeding them is fantastic, but the calling is higher, the task is greater.

If God is not sought on behalf of these people; if the sick, the broken, the lonely and the oppressed are not being prayed for by Salvationists, is what we do enough? For our communities it is the church that is the beacon of light. Be the 'lighthouse of prayer' your community desperately needs, and be the change you want to see.

> 'The price of a single life is huge. The currency is prayer.
> The cost is massive but the prize is glorious. A life for a life.'
> (Written late one night in Reading, UK, 24/7 Prayer 'Boiler Room')
>
> *- Pete Greig, Red Moon Rising (2003) pp.41*

It's crucial that we never forget that we've got God, and everyone else needs to get God. They need our prayers—it's a matter of life and death. People may never know you are praying for them.

Your city council may never realise the corps down the road is praying for their wisdom.

The addicted down by the train station may never realise you are praying for their freedom.

The young woman from welfare may never know you are praying for her salvation.

This is grace—to understand that you are doing for someone what they may never even want to do for you; to pray for someone, deserving or not.

This is grace—we need to walk in it and our neighbourhoods need to be drenched in it; that job belongs to you.

May your corps be not only a lighthouse, but also an outward shining, eternally focused, grace spreading, interceding and above all powerful lighthouse of prayer that changes lives.

Brainstorm

My vision—public lighthouses of prayer

To see every church be a sanctuary in their community with an open 24/7 prayer room, where members of the community are able to come in and seek prayer. This would accomplish a great challenge, to make our churches 'public lighthouses that shine outwardly, not private places merely shining on the inside'.

At my home corps in Box Hill, Melbourne, we recently finished a week of 24/7 prayer. We transformed a room in our building into a sanctuary and God used it to deeply impact everyone who entered. It was comfortable, clean, quiet, located deep within the building, and it was always full of Christians—an awesome, powerful and transformative private lighthouse of prayer.

If we are to be the radical people of God that Jesus would have us be, we need to go one giant, bold step further, and be a public lighthouse of prayer:

One that gives light to the entire community, not just the entire congregation.

A place where not only Christians can come and encounter the God they know, but where the lost can come and encounter him for the first time.

Not only places of reconnection, but places of salvation.

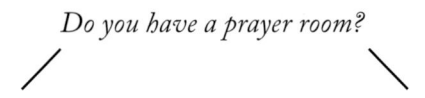

Do you have a prayer room?

If not, can you get one?

If yes... start!
- » Where can it go?
- » What do you need to make it work?
- » Who do you need to get approval from?

If not, can you change your mind?
- » Can you team up with another church?
- » How else can your corps be a lighthouse of prayer to the community?

If yes, is it public or private?

If it's public—awesome. Now evaluate it.
- » Have you seen good fruit?
- » Has there been salvation?

If it's private—awesome. Now, how can you make it public?
- » What logistics do you need to consider?
- » How can you get your corps on board?

Tips:

» Having a week of 24/7 prayer is an awesome way to start—see the chapter on 24/7 prayer for information, or Google '24/7 prayer' for a variety of websites worldwide.
» Need inspiration? Check out *Red Moon Rising* by Pete Greig (the founder of 24/7 prayer) for stories of how public lighthouses of prayer have changed individuals and entire towns. It's available from Word and Koorong.
» Don't think your corps can sustain a prayer room? Team up with other corps (or churches from other denominations) that have caught the fire, and sustain one together.
» Employ a part-time worker, or volunteer, to maintain the prayer room.

Ideas:

» Start prayer meetings before your services.
» Build a culture of bold prayer in your youth.
» Practise praying for people in services, not merely at the mercy seat, but throughout the church.
» Practise laying hands on people.
» Dare to pray for the sick and the bound.
» Practise intercession in your services and prayer meetings.
» Read up on prayer and learn all you can.
» Practise prayer.

134   One Day...

Vision 22 – Prayer destinations

'…that we would have numerous prayer destinations where people could go for prayer retreats, learning opportunities and resources.'

Major Frank Daniels

It is my dream that there be a centre for Christian spirituality set up by the Army in every state in Australia. I am convinced that if we are going to see our mission intentions (caring for people, transforming lives, making disciples, reforming society) fulfilled, we need to deepen our relationship with God.

Any mission we are engaged in, any ministry we perform—if it is going to be successful—must come out of our spirituality. Spirituality is our relationship with God and our spiritual work is fostering that relationship. The 14th century German mystic Meister Elkhart reminds us that, 'Spiritual work involves learning to cooperate with God'.

We cooperate with God when we open up our lives to him through prayer, meditation and silence.

A centre for Christian spirituality would have sleeping accommodation for up to 12 people, a prayer room/chapel, a sitting room and two rooms where the ministry of spiritual direction would be offered.

Therefore I dream of a day when all officers and soldiers of this territory avail themselves of one retreat day every month and one week every year to do some spiritual work.

The centre would offer a day retreat program where officers, soldiers and employees would come and share in some reflective worship, be given a talk on various subjects (such as prayer, silence, meditation, holiness, the life of Christ etc.) and then have time to be on their own for silent prayer and meditation on the given talk.

Up to 10 people could be accommodated for five days to participate in a silent retreat. Each bedroom would have its own ensuite, home-cooked meals would be provided and the participants would be waited upon.

I dream that at the centre, teaching about prayer and holiness of life would be the main focus. Different modes of prayer: vocal—prayer of the lips, meditation—prayer of the mind; contemplation—prayer of the heart would be taught and experienced. Daily prayer would be offered each morning and evening. Taize prayers would be held each Friday night.

I dream of weekly traditional holiness meetings, with a guest band and songster brigade participating, with testimonies shared and the doctrine of full salvation taught.

I dream that officers and soldiers would go to the centre to receive the ministry of spiritual direction.

What is the meaning of my life? How do I integrate all of my life experience? What is God calling me to be and do? What is prayer all about?

These are some of the questions asked in spiritual direction. Spiritual direction helps us engage these and other questions which surface in our longings to live fully, and freely within God's will. It is learning to listen to the depths of who we are and, in discovering who we are, also coming to discover God.

I dream of a day when we have officers and soldiers trained in the art of spiritual direction.

I dream that the spirituality centre would be a destination for 24/7 prayer, where prayer seminars would be conducted and training in prayer companions be given. It would be a resource and training centre from which people would go back to their corps and centres and engage in these ministries.

Brainstorm

- » Do you pray regularly? Is it a refreshing discipline for you? Where do you pray?

- » Is there a place set aside in your corps for prayer?

- » If so, is it used? Could it be improved?

- » If not, discuss where a prayer room might be made, and how it might look and work.

- » Have you ever thought of going on a spiritual retreat? Discuss.

- » What do you make of the dream for a weekly holiness meeting?

- » Try asking yourself the spiritual direction questions each day for a month. Report back to each other (in your group) as to how the exercise is progressing. At the end of the month, discuss where you might go from there.

Vision 23 – Imaginative systems

'…that our systems would be less restrictive and more imaginative to accommodate the new things God wants to do among us.'

John Dalziel

There is a challenge here. If we change our systems many fear we will undermine the values of The Salvation Army. At the heart of our movement we believe we should love God and our neighbour as ourselves.

Our systems need to change so that this belief remains relevant to today's society. In the words of Isaiah 43: 'God wants to do a new thing'. We want to make sure our systems are always ready to respond to this invitation.

Here are a few ways we can make this happen.

Exclusive language is unfitting for today. Our Bible readings, songs, sermons, letters, newsletters and conversations need to use inclusive language.

Our statistics do not record all the good things that are happening. We need the number and backgrounds of the refugees that are assisted, the abused women and children who seek our help, the addicted who come not only to our rehabilitation centres but to all our centres, the teenagers seeking spiritual solutions as distinct from those becoming soldiers, the use of our buildings by community groups that are working in parallel with us.

Many Salvo centres are encouraging numerous community activities that were unheard of a generation ago. Many are open every day and all day, yet our statistics do not record this transformation.

Appropriate computer programs are available to help bring us up-to-date statistics for good, prompt decision making, rather than acting years later when events overwhelm us.

We encourage new people to come to our corps but don't acknowledge that, while the desire for a spiritual life is as strong as it ever was, we live in a different culture from a generation ago. Education, wealth, the age of marriage, attitude to authority and religion have all transformed over time.

There are, however, certain behaviours that are not Christian—such as injustice, malice or arrogance. These behaviours are outward signs of a person not committed to the Christian way.

Our teaching should reflect these changes of emphasis when discussing the priorities of a spiritual life, so that becoming a Christian is seen as a first step in becoming a soldier.

A key part of the lieutenant commitment is service for a set period of years. Let us consider seven year terms for officers as a reflection of the way all careers are now perceived, so that officers are not asked to sign something that could later cause them pain in renouncing.

Fundraising is a vital part of our movement, not just for the finances it raises, but also for the opportunity donors have to participate in our mission. However, the door knock, which is the public face of the Red Shield Appeal, represents less than 10 percent of our income. Why not let the corps and social centres know how much is raised from direct donations to the PR department in their area, as this represents the true result of all our combined fundraising.

To make our fundraising more responsible, why not arrange for local businesses and individuals to have the opportunity to support specific work and report back to them on their 'investment'?

We need systems that encourage all Salvationists to embrace the cosmos and the need to care for our planet. It was part of early 'orders and regulations' and now, when the world has caught up with those early high ideals, we might be slipping. Let us be responsible for God's creation.

Finally, every issue raised here should apply throughout Australia. At present we are divided into two territories and the days for this being a useful administrative system are long gone. The Salvation Army would be better administered as one Australia-wide territory.

When we communicate nationwide through the media. make a public statement or propose a position on a key social issue, it should be presented as one Army view so that we don't lose credibility with the public and government.

We also lose many millions of dollars in wasted administrative costs by having two parallel territorial structures.

Brainstorm

- » Some of these issues are larger than the Salvation War on our local fronts. But not all of them.

- » Locally, how can we make our corps more inclusive to those unaccustomed to Salvationism and Christianity?

- » How can we more effectively and accurately track some of the good things happening on our front?

- » How does adherent membership fit into our plans?

- » How can we effectively stand for justice issues locally and trans-locally?

- » How can we convey the principles of Salvationism to a culture that is nearly completely non-Christian?

- » For the issues relating to the larger Salvation Army, consider discussing those raised in this chapter (eg. financial accountability and territorial consolidation) and then writing letters to your divisional commander (and copying the territorial commander also).

144 One Day...

Vision 24—Marked by holiness

***'… that as a movement we would be marked by
holiness in corporate and individual praxis.'***

Major Helen Brunt

Honestly, when you hear the word holiness, what initially springs to mind?

Impossible dream? Guilt—not there yet? Being separated from the world? Wholeness? Integrity? Being like Jesus? I wish?

What is holiness and how may it shape our lives—individually, in our communities and as a movement?

It is clear that this part of the vision is linked to the previous chapter. Holiness is not static or legalistic. It's dynamic, life-giving and attractive in its straightforwardness and lack of pretence. It has as its basis honouring God by action, passion and choice—both individually and corporately.

Micah 6:8 (NIV) has something to show us here. 'What does the Lord require of you but to do justice, to love mercy and to walk humbly with your God'.

It is firmly grounded in action—doing justice, passion—loving mercy (kindness) and in choices—choosing to walk humbly with God.

The Dream is that these qualities be seen in our individual living, in the communities we belong to and in our movement.

In their book, *Authentic Fair Dinkum Holiness for Ordinary Christians*, Geoff and Kalie Webb refer to Christian Schwarz's insight that the various graces referred to in Galatians 5:22 flow from the main one—love. Hence a translation could read: 'but the fruit of the spirit is love: joy, peace, patience, kindness, goodness, faithfulness, gentleness and self-control.'

These graces then become the marks of holiness expressed by individuals and reflected in our communities, as well as in the structures that are a necessary part of our movement.

How can we move toward the goal of holiness?
1. By checking our behaviour against the graces listed above.
2. By consciously questioning the unthinking assumptions that underlie our practices e.g. by looking at our (usually subconscious) inclusion and exclusion criteria that may well divide our world into 'us and them', with the assumption that those inside are the saints and those outside the

sinners, to whom the gospel message is primarily addressed!

3. Corporately, in ethical and respectful management of people and resources, encapsulating the highest ethical standards of respect for the environment and creation. Moving far beyond the bottom line of financial considerations or protection of the brand name in decision making that is the hallmark of many business enterprises.

If we are serious about moving towards holiness as a movement then we may need to keep examining our use and misuse of power, both individually and corporately.

Choosing to walk humbly with God requires a deliberate setting aside of power and its seduction, a focussed and deliberate questioning of all unthinking assumptions that would seek to distract us from that humble walk.

Friends recovering from addictions remind us that it is far easier to 'talk the talk' than to 'walk the walk'.

Could it be that we also need to re-examine our liking for respectability and our concern with appearances and being religious?

Could it be that in the midst of our daily lives, not just in Christian community, we will continue to hear that call to holiness, wholeness and integrity? We may find it is an integral part of an exciting, challenging and never boring journey with the God of infinite love, wisdom and creativity.

Brainstorm

You may like to choose from the following tasks individually or as a group.

- » When you hear the word holiness—what words or phrases come to mind?

- » Draw a holy person.

- » Brainstorm 10 words to describe a holy community and then rank them in order of importance to you or to your group.

- » Write a charter for a holy corporation.

- » Share a story from daily life when you became aware of the holy in everyday life in an unexpected way.

One Day...

Vision 25 – Outpouring of the Spirit

'…that there would be such an outpouring of the Spirit upon us that we would be courageous and effective witnesses in our families, communities, cities, Australia and the world.'

Lieutenant Rowan Castle

Brothers and sisters, we are The Salvation Army—mobilised and unified towards the common cause of the salvation of the world and it is the Spirit's coming that empowers the believer for this task. Acts 1:8 says, 'But you will receive power when the Holy Spirit comes on you; and you will be my witnesses in Jerusalem, and in all Judea and Samaria, and to the ends of the earth.'

What is the catalyst for this outpouring? What is God waiting for? Surely the God who so loves the world that he sacrifices his only son is not reluctant or preoccupied. Is there some special time for revival? Of course not, what he waits for is you.

He waits for a heart, mind and spirit totally surrendered and available to him. He waits for people who value the salvation of souls and the growth of his kingdom more than personal pride, gain and acceptance.

Much has been said, written and discussed on the topic of evangelism and it sometimes seems that evangelism is something that was possible once but is now rare. Our history as a movement suggests that we were once a revolution of evangelical zeal, methodology and results. Our status as such has now been lost in the face of enormous societal change. Questions of 'Who are we now' and 'What is our purpose' have haunted Salvationists of late as we simply fail to believe that we can experience a revival akin to our early days (e.g. 1878-1888 in England).

We cannot afford to give into the enemy's lie that when it comes to our witnessing we have had our day. Yes, the early days of the Army, and the world in which they lived, have come and gone but we can never afford to accept that the power and truth of Acts 1:8 are also gone. We can never dismiss the promise of Jesus: '...you will receive power when the Holy Spirit comes on you; and you will be my witnesses...'. That same power is available to you today and the key word is 'you'. Not 'we' or 'us', or even 'the Army'—but you!

You can know the Spirit's power. You can be God's witness to the end of the earth. It starts with your consecration to God and ends in his power made manifest in you. There is no program, invitation, permission, better time or better person than you.

So this is what I understand about being a courageous and effective witness. First, some people say 'yes' and some people say 'no'. Our witness must be courageous. There is a risk of failure, rejection and frustration—people will accept Jesus, but others will reject him.

In Mark 4, Jesus promises a one in four ratio; in Luke 17:17, Jesus only gets one out of 10, and in Luke 10:16 Jesus reminds us that it is him who is rejected—not us. Some may say 'no', but we keep going for those who say 'yes'.

Second, people love to hear the good news. Romans 1:16 says, 'I am not ashamed of the gospel, because it is the power of God for the salvation of everyone who believes.' I am constantly amazed (though I shouldn't be surprised) at how people respond to the gospel when it is heard. This good news to which we are a witness is music to humanity's ears.

And finally, the world is crying out for holy people—a people cleansed from sin and filled with love; a people full of grace and free from hypocrisy; a people whose capacity for acceptance stamps out the fear of judgment; a people who are consecrated, fully surrendered and available to God…a people who know the outpouring of the Spirit in their lives.

Brainstorm

» Who is there in your life you can take a risk with today?

» If you wanted to tell someone about Jesus what would you say? Maybe you could take a few moments to think about what you would witness to.

» Take some moments each morning to listen to what God says about the people in your life that don't yet know him. Maybe listen on their behalf and see if God has a message for them.

» Be radical, hit the streets and start your adventure as an evangelist by asking people if they know about Jesus. It can work!

Vision 26 – Global compassion

'…that our compassion would be large enough to be understood as authentically global throughout what we do at home and abroad.'

Commissioner K. Brian Morgan

The authentic always challenges the artificial or superficial!

Our Lord Jesus Christ had little time for 'the performance of religion' rather than 'heart love for God' and strongly challenged those whose profession of godliness was not matched by sincere love and compassionate action in community (Matthew 23:27–28; Luke 11:39–42).

Our tradition and experience as Salvationists is strongly anchored in the teaching and example of Jesus, who saw passionate love for God expressed in active love for others (Matthew 22:37–39).

Salvationists are a 'heart to God' people—redeemed, forgiven, holy and sold out in service as we reflect the likeness of Jesus in everyday life.

We are a 'hand to man' (others) people. Our holiness reaches out with the hands and feet of God's grace that speaks volumes for authentic, compassionate Christian living across the global community.

All that, however, is high-sounding rhetoric unless God's love so grips and motivates us that the artificial is replaced by the authentic in personal witness and action.

Any tendency to isolate ourselves from the real issues of human life and struggle—be it local or global—must be strongly resisted. Loving of our neighbour involves informed minds, practical spirituality, Holy Spirit sensitivity and compassionate action—action that regards sacrifice as privilege and cost as investment in the global mission of our God. Disciples of the Lord Christ live out the challenge to live constantly in the spirit of self-denial and do so with a joyous heart! (Matthew 16:24–26).

The values of the world around us may suggest that 'to have and to hold' equals security, that to hoard our material resources is to guarantee future wellbeing. Such values or attitudes are opposite to the teachings of Jesus who encourages us to invest ourselves sacrificially in the work of the kingdom as we practise authentic global compassion.

The damning result of selfish prosperity is limited vision, diminished willingness to get on board with God's will to see all persons whole, stunted passion for the lost and needy and a refusal to be at God's disposal.

William Booth stated that the evangelical and social emphasis of The Salvation Army is like Siamese (conjoined) twins. He refused to acknowledge our social mission apart from the transforming power of the gospel. Proclamation of God's 'good news' can never be divorced from service. To preach the gospel is to live it.

To close our eyes, ears and hearts to the needs of the world because of local demand is to deny our responsibility, privilege and duty as stewards of all that God entrusts to us.

Compassion and authenticity must always be expressed in a way that is specific to the environment in which we find ourselves. This requires of us a willingness to adapt, to be flexible in approach and understanding of people and places that cry out to us to alleviate injustice, poverty and discrimination.

Sympathy alone is not enough, for this can be cold and formal and without personal engagement. Authentic compassion requires action with empathy without the expectation of plaudits. It does not shrink from the uncomfortable challenge or need the protection of the familiar.

Within the framework of authentic compassion key principles are adhered to that provide the framework for action.

To allow ourselves to become swamped by local or global need is to deny the truth that we can make a difference one life at a time, one issue at a time, one challenge at a time.

Our Founder desired his arms—the arms of the evolving global Salvation Army—to be wide enough to reach around the world and we are part of that desire in action.

Brainstorm

Discussion

- How can we resist the tendency to isolate ourselves from the real issues of human life and struggle on the local and global scene?
- The damning result of selfish prosperity is limited vision. What steps can we take personally, and as an international Salvation Army, to address this?
- Do we, as a Christian church, engage with local government or other community groups in understanding and addressing the paramount needs of our community?
- Does the volume of global need intimidate us? Refugees, sex trafficking, exploitation of workers, famine, disease—how can authentic compassion cope?

Action

- Support local and global mission teams who address specific, documented needs.
- Consider formation of your own mission team.
- Plan now to sacrificially support the annual self-denial appeal.
- Get involved in some down-to-earth local project that benefits the needy or disadvantaged in your community.

Resources
- » *The Salvation Army Year Book*
- » Partners in mission information available through THQ or DHQ
- » World mission fellowship monthly newsletters
- » *All the World* publication, published by IHQ
- » Media outlets that bring local and global issues into our homes
- » People engaged in groundbreaking compassionate activity

Vision 27 – Responsive to the voice of God

***'…that our people would be quick to respond to the
voice of God for whatever he calls them to.'***

Fleur Hodge

I remember as a child, falling asleep on my mother's lap during the holiness meeting. I would wake with my ear on her chest, hearing her voice clearly above the noise of the band's last song and post-meeting chatter.

I think of this as I read about Jesus and his father in the first chapter of John's gospel: 'No one has ever seen God. But his only son, who is himself God, is near to the father's heart; he has told us about him' (1:18).

The Amplified Bible speaks of Jesus being in the bosom of the father, in his intimate presence. His ear rests against the chest of his father. It is from this position that he lives his whole life on earth. Importantly for us, this intimacy doesn't turn his focus inward. On the contrary, it catapults him into a world in need of full salvation.

Jesus' senses are conditioned to kingdom come. He is constantly responding to the father's lead, watching and listening, then joining in (John 5:20). It is important for us to recognise this. Jesus was not a random do-gooder. He was in tune with the father and moved in response to his promptings. This is not to say that Jesus was a robot. No, his obedience was birthed out of his intimacy with the father and their common mission in the world they created—salvation.

As Salvationists, this too is our common mission. This means we must assume our Saviour's posture. In fact this beautiful picture of intimacy in John's gospel extends to include us. At the last supper, we see the disciple Jesus loves, reclining next to Jesus with his head on his chest (John 13:23). It is the mission posture of the coming church; we lay our head against the chest of Christ as he in turn rests his head in the bosom of the father.

This is our posture as soldiers ready to fight against the enemy of souls. We must crawl into the lap of Jesus, where we can be alert to his smallest movement and respond. With our ear pressed to his chest we will hear the urgency in even his faintest whisper.

There is no doubt that he asks for immediate action. He says to us, 'All of us must quickly carry out the tasks assigned to us by the one who sent me, because there is little time left before night falls and all work comes to an end' (John 9:4).

Our response speed is integral to seeing the salvation of the whole world. This involves both 'chronos' and 'chairos' time, the latter of which I know as 'the zone'. It's all about kingdom timing. Unfortunately, I flit in and out of 'the zone', but Jesus lived there! His words and miracles set off spiritual chain reactions because he was responding to the father's promptings.

But this kind of Holy Spirit slipstream wasn't just reserved for Jesus. We see his followers, like Peter, Philip and Paul, with their ears to his chest, all enjoying the same kind of results.

God is dreaming of a Salvation Army sitting on his lap, with our ear to his chest, hearing his heartbeat, listening to his voice telling us what he is doing, asking us to join in so that we can enter into his Holy Spirit slipstream and see the salvation of the whole world. The father longs for soldiers, who like his son, will live in ready response to his voice and who will give whatever it takes to see it done.

> Then in fellowship sweet
> We will sit at his feet,
> Or we'll walk by his side in the way;
> What he says we will do,
> Where he sends we will go,
> Never fear, only trust and obey.
> *- J. H. Sammis, Song 397, The Song Book of The Salvation Army*

Brainstorm

So how can we become an Army that is nestled in the lap of Jesus, listening for His every word? How can we, junior soldier, soldier, cadet and officer alike, posture ourselves to hear the voice of God and respond to it immediately?

We desperately need to learn to hear the voice of God distinctly both individually and corporately. Many of us have never been taught to do so and battle along in an appalling manner. We need to teach our corps' to tune their ears to distinguish the voice of God. This is not a job for the corps officer but the responsibility of every believer. We need to hear the Lord speaking directly to us. This is where the fuel for mission comes from, intimacy with Jesus. When we hear him speaking directly to us, it is more difficult to say no.

So how do you get started? Get a group of keen soldiers together and commit to walk this journey together. Intimacy with Jesus is personal but not private. This is where we have fallen down. We stopped asking each other, 'How's your soul?'. We need to start to make listening to Jesus an integral part of our gatherings as well as our individual daily rations.

There are many excellent resources to help. I would recommend *Can You Hear Me: Tuning Into a God Who Speaks* by Brad Jersak. This book revolutionised my prayer-life both individually and corporately. He's also written a children's book called *Children Can You Hear Me?*. This is a must for every Sunday school teacher and junior soldier sergeant who wants to train up warriors who are ready to win the world for Jesus.

Here's an easy exercise to tune your ears to the voice of God. First, close your eyes and imagine your fridge; open it up and see what you have in there. Could you do it? Yes, that means your imagination is working just fine. Jesus wants to use your imagination to speak with you.

So close your eyes again and imagine a place you feel safe, maybe a real place or an imagined one. When you can see it, look around and find Jesus there. He's there, he told you he would never leave you or forsake you, even in your imagination. When you see him, go over and listen to what he says, maybe he will give you something or do something. I find it best to write these things down as it is amazing how quickly you forget.

You can also do this for others. You can take them to Jesus in your imagination and watch and listen on their behalf, then share with them what you saw and heard. This is a wonderful way to encourage our brothers and sisters in Christ. You can even use it for people who don't know Jesus yet. It can be a powerful way to bring people into the kingdom. It's a way of listening to God and hearing what he would have you do.

As you become adept at hearing his voice, you won't even need to close your eyes anymore. God will highlight people and things to you, to show what he's up to, and whisper directions to guide you. This is the Salvation Army I dream about. One that is so close to Jesus that he can whisper his heart's desire for one of his lost ones and without a second's thought, we go to them with a word for them from the Saviour that melts their resistance and ushers them into the kingdom.

Let this be our prayer.

> If on my soul a trace of sin remaineth,
> If on my hands a stain may yet be seen,
> If one dark thought a wearied mind retaineth,
> O wash me, Lord, till every part be clean.
> For I would live that men may see Thyself in me,
> I would in faith ascend Thy holy hill,
> And with my thoughts in tune with Thy divinity,
> Would learn how best to do Thy holy will.
>
> *– Chorus 118, The Song Book of The Salvation Army*

Vision 28 – Unusual response of the called

'…that our officer training programs would be taxed by the unusual response of the called to serve as officers in The Salvation Army.'

Major Marney Turner

As I read the words of the territorial commander's vision and dream, the Holy Spirit leads me to Ezekiel 37 and reminds me that we as a territory could be (like Ezekiel) receiving a 'prophetic view' of what the Lord sees in our midst at this time in our history.

God leads Ezekiel out into a valley of dry bones—this God inspired vision mirrors Israel's situation at that time. Conquered by Babylon, exiled from their land, cut off from their centre of worship, the Israelites were as spiritually dry as they could be. God required the prophet to see the world through his eyes, to see those truths that cannot always be seen by mere human perception, nor exacting intellectual application.

The truth was that at this time, God's people were not where they were called to be. They were not quick to respond to the voice of God and his call upon their lives. The consequences of their disobedience brought a 'valley of exceedingly dry bones'

(Ezekiel 37:2). Dark nights, dry souls, brittle bones, no tears of repentance, bleakness, certainly no resources and definitely desolation—no life whatsoever.

But, into the midst of this valley comes God's question to Ezekiel (37:3)—mission (im)possible?—'Son of man, can these bones live? O Sovereign Lord, you alone know.' The great 'I am' asks this prophet what he sees, thinks and believes.

To our minds, the question seems impossible to answer. Literally and metaphorically, Ezekiel must know that these bones cannot live. Dry bones are dead; they do not live again. The House of Israel was dead! At this time they were as far removed from spiritual vitality as they could be. Yet God set the stage for the miraculous response to an impossible question, and situation.

This is what I believe God is doing in our territory right now. In our journey of faith he is preparing this territory for a miraculous response of obedience to God's perfect will, not merely satisfied with settling for obedience to his permissive will. Can we, as God's Army, really be quick to respond to the voice of God for whatever, wherever, whenever he calls us to do and to be?

Can we really take Jesus' terms of discipleship as the benchmark for our own passionate obedience to his calling, as clearly outlined in Mark 8:34–35: 'Whoever desires to come after me, let them deny themselves, take up their cross, and follow me. For whoever desires to save their life will lose it, but whoever loses their life for my sake and the gospel's will save it.'

As we read on, Jesus has a whole lot more to say about what being an authentic disciple of Jesus really involves.

With the territorial commander, I dare to dream, believe, pray, preach, work and witness to this wonderful, compelling call. I dare to have a vision that God's people will be quick to respond to his voice for whatever he calls them to.

I dare to believe that God's officer training programs will be taxed by the unusual response of the called to serve as officers in The Salvation Army. The valley of small excuses, small vision and small ambitions needs to be given up if the bones of this territory are to live.

We must continue to have anointed, appointed, 'covenanted' officers who will, for Jesus' sake, lead this Army into victory for God's kingdom.

God, help us to be faithful and obedient and to take up our prophetic mantle fighting for social justice and mission to the urban and city's poor. God, help us to keep our soldier's commitment to holiness and costly discipleship and to be quick to respond with 'Yes, yes, yes' to Jesus.

This is what I see and what I dream—Ezekiel 37:12–14, 'Therefore prophesy and say to them, thus says the Lord God: Behold, O my people, I will open your graves and cause you to come up from your graves and bring you into the land of Israel. Then you will know that I am the Lord, when I have brought you up. I will put my Spirit in you, and you shall live, and I will place you in your own land. Then you shall know that I the Lord, have spoken it and performed it, says the Lord.'

On our feet, living, moving and having our being in Jesus! Just do it—now, now, now!

Brainstorm

» From dark nights to God's miraculous revival of an Army of loving, obedient, warriors—how does this transition take place in your life, your place of worship, work and community?

» When the Spirit breathes on his Army, it will be an Army with a mission heart, informed minds and a prophetic voice. How do we allow this process to occur in our midst? Are you willing to let Jesus truly be Lord?

» We need to surrender to a radical obedience, to the direction of God found through his Word and his Spirit regardless of the damage it may cause our reputation or any other dearly held icon. What is your response to this dream be?

» In order to be responsive and quick to God's voice we need to be on our faces in prayer. How is your prayer life?

One Day...

Vision 29 – The priesthood of all believers

'…that our local officers would be so empowered to understand their foundational role in the corps ministries and fully embrace the priesthood of all believers.'

Anthony Castle

How do you structure an army? Where do the personnel fit? Should officers be at the front of the battle, dodging fire at the frontlines? If so, what do all the soldiers do? Plan the attack?

No. An army structured like this would never take any ground or defeat the enemy. It's common sense that the frontline of battle is the officers' responsibility, but it is not their sole appointment. The soldiers fight at the frontlines; the officers plan strategy. Officers are present, but not immediate, to the battle.

It's no different in The Salvation Army. God has given our movement a militaristic identity that functions with a system of ranks and a structure that requires different personnel in different roles. The Salvation Army has officers and soldiers and our corps' ministries are the frontlines of a war—the war against the powers of darkness! (Ephesians 6:12). We need to make sure our army is structured properly and our officers and soldiers are in the right places.

Just as military officers plan the battle and oversee the attack, so our local officers prepare, establish and support the work in our corps. In our army structure, the role of local officers is foundational to our corps and its ministries.

It is also the role of our local officers to be creatively and aggressively planting new and effective ways to advance the kingdom. We need them to be discerning the best approaches, overseeing their application and keeping them accountable. Present, but not immediate, to the battle.

Imagine if a local officer set up a soup-run for the corps to minister to the neighbourhood's homeless and destitute. Do we then expect our officers to make the soup, butter the sandwiches, drive the van, serve the coffee, hand out the blankets and preach the good news of Jesus several nights a week all by themselves?

No. This certainly wouldn't be helping our officers in their apostolic role (Acts 6:2-4). But what if we do find our officers alone in the frontlines of battle? How can we empower officers to better understand their role?

Well, it's quite simple. Only soldiers can empower their officers to work in their foundational role and they do this in two ways: by being part of the corps' ministry and by doing what the officers ask.

For soldiers, this is not just a matter of 'helping the officers', this is our calling and commitment. What do the *Articles of War* suggest? Absolute and total devotion to the kingdom's work. As soldiers we are welcome, if not obliged, to preach, work, pray, volunteer, exorcise, heal, advocate and evangelise. What better place to do this than our corps' ministries.

For officers to work in a foundational role, they must do two things. First, ask the soldiers to go to the frontlines and, second, trust them with their orders. This is how any army is structured, and our army has long practised and preached the 'priesthood of all believers' (1 Peter 2:9). Our *Articles of War*—the covenant that binds our army together—is a testimony that all in this movement, officers and soldiers alike, are able to serve God with their gifts.

Now, I'm not suggesting that officers can't get their hands dirty in the thick of the fight, or that soldiers should be forced to work in areas contrary to their giftings. I am suggesting that soldiers be released to live out the calling of their covenant in their corps ministries. Only then will our local officers be so empowered to function in their strategic, apostolic role. And only when our officers and soldiers are working in the right roles within our corps will The Salvation Army be unleashed to share God's love, defeat the powers of darkness and tear hell's throne to pieces.

Brainstorm

Soldiers

- » Have you looked for where you are needed?
- » Have you asked your officers where you are needed?
- » Have you asked Jesus where you are needed?

Officers

- » Does the corps need more discipleship?
- » Do your soldiers need specific training?
- » Could you have more soldiers? Do you need to run recruits classes?

One Day...

Vision 30 – A sparkling, refreshing 'cocktail'

'…that our women would have appointments and responsibilities commensurate with their gifts, abilities and experience.'

Major Robyn Clinch

Can this dream ever be fully realised? Is it a possibility? One of the best things about grassroots ministry is when men and women are passionately committed to seeing God's kingdom happen here on earth. The dream is happening! Women and men are using their gifts and passions to serve as senior local officers at corps and are involved in heading up ministry activities as well as leading as corps officers.

Similarly, in the extensive social work of the Army, there are extremely capable men and women heading up not only departments, but the networks themselves. When this happens there is often a sparkling, refreshing 'cocktail' as each member of the team— gender aside—leads in his or her area of giftedness. It is the way things should be. It is the Genesis story before the 'fall'. It is then not just a dream; it is a God-glorifying reality.

But the cocktail becomes bland and flat when all the ingredients aren't included. When women are not involved—not using their gifts and not recognised alongside their brothers as having a meaningful contribution to make—the dream becomes a demeaning fairytale and a poor substitute for the glorious founding vision.

The cocktail can start to sour for officers once the appointment is made for divisional or territorial leadership and especially at executive leadership level.

While we uphold, deservedly esteem and eagerly emulate the likes of the Generals Evangeline Booth and Eva Burrows—two lone females in the group of 16 generals of the Army—we also recognise that they were single women.

Would a married woman ever be given the opportunity to lead in such a way? It is highly unlikely, unless international cultural barriers are vigorously tackled and opposed. And while we can easily respond to joint leadership at a corps level for dual clergy couples (both are now designated simply as 'corps officers'), can't we dream of the day when we similarly have territorial commanders jointly leading?

Dream of the day when female officers are no longer referred to as 'the divisional commander's wife' (and they no longer feel the temptation to punch the bestower of such a title!).

Dream of the day when women are not automatically appointed to the women's ministry department and receive 'figurehead' appointments, irrespective of passions and gifting.

Dream of the day when women are no longer treated as neither invisible nor negligible.

Dream of the day when talented independent officers are not allowed to become redundant, regardless of a spouse's appointment.

For such dreams to be achieved, any male-dominated culture needs to be challenged and barriers broken down. It means that we will all put in the hours needed in bringing God's kingdom now. It means that practical family tasks are shared in such a way that dual-clergy couples are able to reach their God-given potential. It means that we will stand firm in the face of ridicule and opposition when we uphold the place of women.

Realisation of this dream means that so much more could be achieved for the kingdom as women are truly released to live out their calling.

Realisation of this dream means that we would have more officers to deploy to the field.

Realisation of this dream means less frustration and hurt, and that more would know the fulfilment and joy that comes from doing what God has uniquely shaped them to do.

Realisation of this dream means we reflect the image of God as described in Genesis and have an understanding of what Paul means when he talks about being 'in Christ'.

Realisation of this dream brings the kingdom even closer as we look for the best and appreciate each other's diverse, deep and rich differences and gifts.

Now, that would become a cocktail worth drinking!

Suggested further reading:

Seasons—A Woman's Calling to Ministry, Major JoAnn Shade, published by Salvation Books, October 2007

Why not Women?, Loren Cunningham, David Joel Hamilton with Janice Rogers, published by YWAM Publishing, 2000

'*Gender Issues and The Salvation Army*' from *Postmodernism and The Salvation Army*, Major Leanne Ruthven (Ed.) published by TSA, Aust Eastern, Aust Southern and NZ, Fiji, Tonga Territories, 2006

'*Married Officer Leadership*', by Major Richard Munn Journal of Aggressive Christianity, Issue 39 Oct–Nov, 2005

Brainstorm:

» What does it mean to be male or female in the sight of God?

» What is the place of women in God's kingdom?

» In corps with married corps officers leading, try saying/thinking 'our officers' instead of 'our officer'. Unless you call your male officer Mr Officer don't demean your female officer by calling her Mrs Officer, or Mrs Captain. She has her own name and rank. Why is this important?

» How many women are represented in decision making groups? How can this be improved?

» Around corps/centres/headquarters, how can we make sure the best person for the job is appointed, regardless of gender?

» How can I stand up for females and ensure their ministry is not eroded?

Vision 31 – Young people filled with the Spirit

'…that our young people would be filled with the Spirit and recognised as contributors in the fight.'

Xander Coleman

At its inception, The Salvation Army was inherently a youth movement—an army of young people. Primitive Salvationists recruited young people who were fresh and energetic to take the Army across the world. It was seen as commonplace for cadets to be commissioned at 16 years of age, or commissioners to be as young as 23.

Commissioner George Scott Railton lead a group of seven young women to invade the United States of America—only one of whom was over 20-years-old! The Army was not afraid of putting young people in leadership positions because it had nothing to lose and everything to gain for the sake of the kingdom of God.

Things have changed a lot since then. Young people have nowhere near as much prominence in Army ministry. True, they still have entire departments dedicated to them at territorial and divisional levels. But it seems that throughout the past century youth ministry has come to mean ministry to youth rather than ministry by youth.

You see dry bones? In Australia, our generation of young people are plagued with influences such as binge drinking, drug abuse, internet pornography, sexual promiscuity, teenage pregnancy, broken families, abused children, divorced parents, depression, suicide. If ever there's been a generation that needs good news, it's this generation. We would be naive to assume that these issues exist exclusively outside our ranks.

And yet, out of this broken generation, God seems to be raising up a remnant of the faithful—and not just faithful because they show up every Sunday. Faithful in surrendering their lives to him; faithful in praying for his kingdom to come on this earth; faithful in trusting in his promise; faithful in holiness, in evangelism, in passion, in commitment, in covenant, in truth—an army of young people who are seeking after him.

God is pouring out his Spirit on young men and young women who will receive him, who will surrender their lives for his kingdom. That old prophecy is stirring, echoing, growing louder, 'your sons and daughters will prophesy'. Can you hear it?

The prophets are stirring, have you heard them (see brainstorm)?

The first fruits are emerging—have you seen them? Teenagers testifying to freedom from the power of sin; teenagers from this territory leading corps outposts in foreign lands; teens moving to rough neighbourhoods so they can share God's love with the residents; teenagers writing books on holiness for other teenagers.

Young people have so much to offer! As a good friend of mine says, there is no junior version of the Holy Spirit. If a young person is gifted in preaching, let her preach. If a pre-teen is gifted in leading worship, let him lead worship. If there are gifted evangelists, prophets, healers, givers, leaders, pastors, teachers—let them do it! May our young people be holy, filled with the Spirit of God, anointed for ministry and mobilised. An army of young people!

> 'And this vision will be. It will come to pass; it will come easily; it will come soon. How do I know? Because this is the longing of creation itself, the groaning of the Spirit, the very dream of God. My tomorrow is his today. My distant hope is his 3D. And my feeble, whispered, faithless prayer invokes a thunderous, resounding, bone-shaking great "Amen!" from countless angels, from heroes of the faith, from Christ himself. And he is the original dreamer, the ultimate winner. Guaranteed.'
>
> *–Pete Greig, The Vision*

Brainstorm

» How do we make it happen? How can we mobilise our young people?

» What sort of role models are we for our young people? Are we modelling holiness, mission-focus and sensitivity to the spirit?

» Research shows that to develop, all children need someone unconditionally committed to them. Spiritually, how can you commit to a young person's development?

» Do you think we expect too much of our young people? Too little? Why?

» Check out *The Vision* by Pete Greig—part poem, part prophecy, part distant hope, part realised dream: www.24-7prayer.com/cm/resources/28

Vision 32 – Authentic child soldiers

'...that our children would be welcomed as authentic soldiers with proper opportunities to celebrate the presence of Christ in their lives and in their environments.'

Lisa Wynne

Do we welcome children as authentic soldiers?

Sometimes I wonder if we do. Do we really support them and help them in their spiritual formation? There is no question that they are important to the kingdom.

Jesus spoke strongly in Matthew 18 regarding this. He said we people should become childlike and redevelop their characteristics of helplessness, dependence, trust, sensitivity to truth and unconditional love. Jesus said we must not cause one of these little children who believe in him to sin. It is our mandate to welcome children—not just our children but all children.

In a world of constant change, children today are exposed to influences from the media, internet, passive signage and their peers. Many parents struggle with their own beliefs and values and hence their children are left to form their own belief and value system.

Research analyst George Barna says that once the worldview of children has been shaped and embraced, they unconsciously strive to make choices that are consistent with their perspective. He claims that by the time a child is 13 years of age the way he or she views the world is already determined.

We as The Salvation Army need to speak the gospel into the lives of as many children as we can. We want all children's worldviews to include a knowledge, understanding and experience of God—Father, Son and Holy Spirit. We want children to have a 'Biblical worldview', meaning the Bible influences their thinking, how they act and what they value.

How as The Salvation Army can we do this?

We need to help children in their spiritual formation and to encourage and equip parents in the discipling of their children. Children need to be able to experience and express their love for God in our services. Children have amazingly strong faith.

We cannot turn children into little adults. They naturally express freedom, liberty, fun and faith that says all things are possible.

May we encourage this and not crush it. May we continually paint a big—in fact a huge—picture of our supernatural God. May children feel loved, valued and have a sense of ownership of their corps.

Children are not the future Army but the Army of today.

It was as a child that many people in full-time service for God received their calling. Children are open to the moving of the Holy Spirit. May we create environments where this can occur and be nurtured.

Samuel clearly heard God's voice. Mary was highly favoured by God and anointed for an amazing responsibility. David fought the enemy in the strength of God and won. What awesome, amazing purposes and plans does God have for our children? May we create and offer environments for them to hear God's voice and know him personally.

The Salvation Army has in place a fundamental structure for the spiritual nurture of children. When children are dedicated to God by their parents, we commit, as a corps, to supporting the family and children in the years ahead. They are then welcomed to the First Steps Ministry.

We give children the opportunity to become junior members of The Salvation Army. Becoming a junior soldier formally recognises their decision to make Jesus Christ Lord and Saviour of their lives. These programs should not become 'just what we do'; we should truly celebrate and rejoice in these things and offer the best discipleship opportunities possible.

May our children always feel comfortable in our worship services.

May we recognise their worth, gifts and abilities in worshipping and serving our God.

Let us give our children opportunity to pray for healing of the sick. Let us give our children opportunity to share their love for God in testimony.Let us give our children opportunity to use their musical talents in worship.

God can use children to speak to the lives of the congregation and not only be spoken to by an adult telling a children's story.

God has a heart for children. May we reflect God's heart for children in our corps, social programs and our communities. Let us welcome children as The Salvation Army of today and appreciate all that they offer to the body of Christ.

Brainstorm

Ways the vision can become reality on your local front

Projects/ideas:
» Visioning day for children's leaders and other corps members.
Sessions for parents/corps members on the importance of discipling children.
Family worship—what does it look like? Children leading worship, not just performing.
Corps prayer points given to children's leaders so children can be part of the corps prayer team.
Junior soldiers modelling small groups. Operate in homes (on a roster) if possible, with parents providing a snack. This helps lead children into youth cells.
» Child representatives on the children's ministry team.
» Children (Sunday school/junior soldiers) serving others in the community, i.e. cleaning, gardening, visiting—especially other children with needs.
» Peer mentoring.
» Children's conference days (girls/boys), celebration worship, electives—prayer, journalling, running a small group etc., and lots of fun.

Resources:
- *Making your Children's Ministry the Best Hour of Every Kids Week*, Sue Miller, 2004, Zondervan
- *Postmodern Children's Ministry*, Ivy Beckwith, 2004, Zondervan
- *Transforming Children into Spiritual Champions*, George Barna, 2003, Regal Books
- *Revolutionary Parenting*, George Barna

Questions:
- What picture of God are we painting for our children?
- As a corps, what are we modelling to our children—what does a Christian look like?
- What should we be modelling to our children?

Vision 33 – Extraordinary forgiveness

'…that an extraordinary forgiveness and healing of past sins and hurts would prevail upon all people victimised by our practices or inattention.'

Barry Gittins

As expressed in that prayer, we dare to dream that those The Salvation Army has wounded, deliberately or inadvertently, will forgive us and be healed.

We know that God is love. We also know God chooses to work predominantly through human agency. So, for our dream to come true, we need to own our part and act accordingly (see action points below).

There are two particular (and often connected) issues that this particular vision for The Salvation Army takes into account: the overwhelming need for reconciliation between indigenous and non-indigenous Australians, and the abuse of children. To help heal these situations, Salvationists can act in accordance with the Biblical teaching of repentance.

As taught by John the Baptist and Jesus himself, repentance is a process; recognising a wrong, feeling and expressing sorrow (in this context, saying sorry) and working to put things right.

Think about reconciliation. Between 1788 and 1850 the United Kingdom transported 162,000 prisoners to this land. A culture of violence and punishment birthed inter-cultural havoc and dispossession. Genocide ensued, interspersed with well-meaning but fatally flawed approaches and policies such as assimilation and integration.

Some ask why the Salvos need to act to help reconcile Aussies, considering the many positive stories of pioneer Salvos working and living with Aboriginal Australians.

The answer, apart from the racist jokes and mindset that were part of Salvationists' culture as little as two decades ago, is summed up in two words: 'stolen generations'.

With all the good will in the world, the Army participated with other churches in removing children forcibly from their parents and communities. Grievous wounds have not yet been healed.

This year marks the 10th anniversary of a statement by The Salvation Army supporting the reconciliation process, advocating land rights and equality for all. We need to breathe life into those fine, just words.

To promote healing, the Army has to accept its past is not free of error, nor is its present. We need to do more, care more; act more boldly and advocate more openly.

The Army did great good for hosts of children separated from parents or loving family. For some deeply scarred children, however, Salvation Army children's homes were not an oasis.

The Army has officially issued an apology some years past, disowning offending parties, cooperating with police enquiries, offering former 'home children' counselling services and financial compensation. This is in line with scriptural repentance. This is God's will.

There are those in the movement who would believe legal liability and fiscal consequences are much more of a priority for the Army than some idealistic dream of accountability, transparency and restitution.

A dream of authentic holiness—that's what Jesus taught and lived.

We worship God in spirit and truth, believing that all that is done in darkness will be seen in God's light—and that the truth will set us free. We must repent to fulfil our dream.

To help heal, we can acknowledge harm and wrong doing, offer sincere sorrow and regret—by saying sorry—and help reconcile broken people through our own actions and lives, in Christ's name and for the sake of us all.

Brainstorm

Reconciliation action points
For individuals:
- As a person, a family group or as part of your church, practise what you preach by supporting National Sorry Day.
- Oppose racist statements whenever they are expressed in your presence.
- Through reading, viewing films and documentaries, listening to musicians and watching performance groups—and through conversations with indigenous Australians—share an understanding of the history and the differences that divide us. Find common ground in the things that unite us.
- Vote with your feet—support community, political and civic leaders who advocate justice and reconciliation.

For the movement:
- In corps, find out what tribes were indigenous to your geographic area and research what happened to drive them out of the area.
- Invite indigenous speakers into your corps, your cell groups and homes.
- Present to your worship community the opportunity to validate a formal recognition of past wrongs.

» Through fundraising and advocacy, offer assistance to Salvationists working with indigenous communities.

Abused children action points

For individuals:

- » Be open to people's hurts and history; validate and help heal their pain by an open and honest discussion.
- » Open your homes to people who have been hurt—invite folks to share a meal and practise genuine listening skills and compassion.
- » Don't turn away from possible abuse situations that come to your attention; be vigilant to guard against the harm of children in your home, your corps, your community.

Vision 34 – Love supremely, rely completely

'…that God would see that we love him supremely through Christ and that our reliance on the Holy Spirit completes his hope in us.'

Major Barbara Wilson

At the heart of the gospel, is an invitation to intimacy with God, sometimes referred to as the Divine Romance. From the beginning, God has always been expressing his love, inviting a response and drawing us into a place of intimacy with him.

The Bible, providing us, as it does, with the foundations of our faith, is not primarily a theological discourse, but rather a book about relationships. Throughout the entire Bible, God's commitment to his people and the covenant relationship to which he invites us, is expressed in love language.

Poignantly captured in the book of Hosea, God is depicted as the adoring and long-suffering husband of Israel, the unfaithful wife. The sublime poetry of Song of Songs records an intimate encounter between the Lover and the Beloved. The Revelation refers to the culmination of all history, when the beautifully adorned 'bride of Christ' is presented to the Bridegroom, and all participants are caught up in the joy of that glorious union, celebrated at the 'marriage supper of the Lamb'.

Speaking of this close relationship, Jesus (in John 14) says, 'I no longer call you servants...I have called you friends (because I've told you everything, there are no secrets)'.

This is the language of intimacy.

Yet history attests the sad possibility of proclaiming and practising the love of God without actually being intimately acquainted with the Divine Lover. One of the saddest images from Scriptures must be the picture of Jesus knocking at the door, not to enter the hearts of unbelievers, but to be part of what is happening in the Church!

In just a few short years, the Church at Laodicea had become 'lukewarm'—somehow they'd lost their passion for God, adopting a 'business as usual' attitude. Jesus' words about dining together (Revelation 3:20) are an invitation to intimacy, suggesting a beautifully presented table, a carefully chosen menu and two people spending unhurried time together—simply enjoying each other's company.

More than anything else, God wants The Salvation Army to love him supremely. Yes, the Army is called to serve—we like to serve, we're good at serving—but over and above anything we may do for God, is an invitation to know him and enjoy him. Our brother Paul, fervently serving all his Christian life, said, 'I want to know Christ,' (Philippians 3:10).

By all accounts, first-generation Salvationists loved God supremely. Some of their conversion stories are thrilling, the transformation of their lives compelling and their single-mindedness inspiring. The lengths to which they went to share this new-found 'love of their lives' were extraordinary and the by-product of this new relationship was joy, unbridled and spontaneous. We must never lose this Salvation Army distinctive.

And God has hopes for us.

> 'Having believed, you were marked in him with a seal, the promised Holy Spirit, who is a deposit guaranteeing our inheritance,'
>
> *- Ephesians1:13,14*

The Spirit indwelling the believer is the mark of the one who claims us as his own; the 'seal' on this close relationship; the down payment with the promise of more to follow.

How blessed we are that the Spirit has come to live with us. How grateful for the guidance, confirmation, illumination, prompting and divine energy he brings into our personal lives and our beloved Army. How reassuring that we do not need to lean on our own understanding, past achievements, good name or limited resources because God's Spirit (whom Jesus called 'the Friend') 'will take you by the hand and guide you' (John 14:26).

As we rely on and co-operate with the Spirit, God's good and holy purposes for The Salvation Army become reality.

Brainstorm

- » Consider the Churches at Laodicea and Ephesus. One had become 'lukewarm', the other had turned away from its 'first love' (Revelation 3:15,16 and Revelation 2:4).
- » Is there any evidence where you are that the Army has become 'lukewarm' or forsaken her 'first love'? (and let's remember 'the Army' is you and me!).
- » What can we do to ensure that The Salvation Army stays true to our 'first love', Jesus?
- » Reflect on John 12:1-3. Notice how Martha, Mary and Lazarus expressed their love to Jesus on this occasion.
- » Ask yourself, 'How do I express my love to Jesus?' (rather than love for Jesus).
- » Remember that an act of pure love brings something into the world that time cannot erase. This is true of Mary's expression of love. Jesus said we would be talking about it long after the event… and we are! (Matthew 26:10-13).
- » Listen to some of the songs from the musical Hosea. Read some of the Scriptures from Hosea as a group. Dwell on verses such as Hosea 2:14 and give thanks for the 'wooing' nature of God's Spirit—'Echoes of mercy, whispers of love' (song 310, *The Song Book of The Salvation Army*).

- Spend time alone and read from Song of Songs 2:8-13. Focus on verse 9. At first, the Lover meets the wall behind which the Beloved is hiding.
- Reflect on an experience in your life when God came seeking a close encounter. If you were hiding, what were the walls you hid behind and how were you released from that?
- Do you still have walls that keep you from intimacy with God?
- Do you see yourself as God's 'beautiful one'?
- Talk about 'joy in The Salvation Army' (or, if you like, sing song 807, *The Song book of The Salvation Army*).
- Early Salvos were known for their joyous approach to life and ministry.
- Where do you see joy in The Salvation Army today?
- Where does joy come from?
- Is your corps, service centre, office… known as a happy place? If it is, good on you—may your joy be infectious! If not, what can you do about it?
- Be honest about your corps, your centre, yourself. We are not very good at self-criticism, confession or repentance. But 'a broken and a contrite heart' can be the way forward to restoration and wholeness.
- Be intentional in Sunday worship to speak to the Lord (not just about the Lord) so we keep the focus where it belongs.

Vision 35 – Expressing our love

'…that God would see that we love him absolutely and are expressing our love for him by our active love for others.'

Commissioner Wesley Harris

It is unfortunate that the English word 'love' is diluted through being too widely used so that it may mean very different things. We say we love chocolate or we love our family or we love God. The Greeks were wiser in that they had different words for different kinds of love.

In the New Testament, a special word for love was 'agape' which meant something more than a passing passion or a slight preference. 'Agape' denoted something deep and abiding. God's love for us is like that, and our love for him should be similar.

But how can such love for God be stirred within us? After all, he is invisible and sometimes his ways are past finding out. That makes our loving him seem hard.

Nonetheless, our love may be engendered by considering his love for us (1 John 4:19). He has showered us with gifts and especially the unspeakable gift of Jesus who was love incarnate. God so loved us that he divested himself of the glories of heaven and came to earth, limited to the span of a baby and restricted by time and space.

We are urged to love the Lord—not in a sporadic or half-hearted manner but with our whole being (Matthew 22:37)—because of the awesome fact that the controlling power of the universe is not an impersonal force, but a father-like God.

Our love for God should be much more than a fuzzy feeling, or an emotional spasm. It should be a settled state of heart and mind and a glad acceptance of the values by which he moves and works. Evidence of such love will be seen in our desire to keep his commandments, not reluctantly but gladly (1 John 5:3).

It will also be seen in our love for our Christian brothers and sisters, recognising that we cannot be right with God and wrong in our attitude towards fellow believers. I can picture the devil dancing with glee when bad relationships creep into the Christian community. He needs 'cutting off at the socks!' (Good people may sometimes disagree, but they should not be disagreeable and we have God's word on that.)

Finally, the validity of our love for God will be proved by our love for the least, the lost and lowest, for whom Jesus died. Every

Salvation Army corps exists for the people who don't belong to it as well as those who do. We are not meant to be merely inward looking. The desire to reach out to others should be in our DNA.

We are called to care and even love the unlovely, and those with whom we may have little natural affinity. Our forebears in the faith had what was called a passion for souls and lamented any Sunday when there were no souls at the Mercy Seat.

Have we become fatally accepting of empty penitent forms and a dearth of converts being brought through to soldiership in God's Army? Shame on us if that is so!

The greatest need is not for improved techniques or clever marketing—helpful though these things may be. The greatest need is for agape, love that is not faked but full, deep and strong, down to earth and as high as heaven.

The Apostle Paul spoke of God pouring out his love into our hearts by the Holy Spirit he has given us (Romans 5:5). May he do just that!

Brainstorm

- Are we loving God absolutely? What are some distractions from such love? How can we get rid of them?

- Are we actively loving others? How?

- Activity—The 28 day experiment.
  a. They say it takes 28 days to start a habit. For 28 days, why not intentionally setting time to express your love to God absolutely and to actively love others?
  b. With comrades in your corps you can be mutually accountable and spur one another on to this love and these good deeds. It can be something under the radar or it can be an official Salvation Army project.
  c. When the 28 days are complete, evaluate what has changed in your love for God, in your love for others, in your corps, and in your neighbourhood. Brainstorm with your group as to what the next step might be. Ask God to show you the sequel to the Dream. One day is coming!

One Day... – In Conclusion

Commissioner Jim Knaggs

> 'Like an open book, you watched me grow from conception to birth; all the stages of my life were spread out before you, the days of my life all prepared before I'd even lived one day.'
> – *Psalms 139:16 (The Message)*

The Dream, for the Australia Southern Territory to live totally in obedience to God, is a hope to be actualised by everyone in the territory, each unit of the body and each person in the fellowship. We are being enjoined to follow the holy purposes and direction of God in an ever-changing world at every level of our lives.

Our world is threatened by the enemy on every front. We must, in the name of Christ, be on guard and active in our endeavours to be salt and light. How else will others 'taste and see that the Lord is good?'

The clear objective is to love God by loving people—all people. That includes bringing them to love Christ (best seen by our own example) in every way. God enables us to love and follow him completely with affect towards our every day, as well as the overarching paradigms that inform our thoughts and actions.

These actions are recognised by our practical concern for people in practical ways and are defined by social programs or issues of social justice. Each of us is called to do something.

This whole concept of 'one day' draws us to the hope and promise of a future with God. Without him we have no future worth anything. It can be seen in the celebration of 1 Peter 1:3–5 (*The Message*):

> 'What a God we have! And how fortunate we are to have him, this Father of our Master Jesus! Because Jesus was raised from the dead, we've been given a brand-new life and have everything to live for, including a future in heaven—and the future starts now! God is keeping careful watch over us and the future. The Day is coming when you'll have it all—life healed and whole.'

One day is coming. It's not just a dream. It is a vision of what God is calling us to be. This is where he is calling us and where he will equip, empower and enable us to go. The point isn't the destination in particular. It is the journey. You and I can glorify him in the process of leading the world to Christ.

There are many thoughts contained within this book that need not be limited to the Australia Southern Territory. Take these possibilities wherever God is leading you. Know that it is about inclusivity, openness and limitlessness in all aspects of your expression of faith. He is able.

Join him and join us. It is God's idea. All of us are at the heart of his plan. We can be The Salvation Army he means us to be. We can—because the 'one day' coming is his dream for us. Hallelujah!

SALVO Publishing Catalogue

Authentic Holiness

Geoff and Kalie Webb tackle Wesleyan holiness from a peculiarly Australian, Salvationist perspective that balances theology and pastoral care in its treatment. This book not only teaches but aims at transformation.

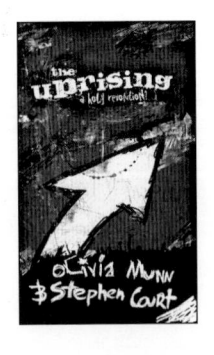

THE UPRISING: A holy revolution?

Teenager Olivia Munn throws this question in the face of youth and then proposes the answer with Stephen Court. Hardcore, uncompromising holiness is the key to an uprising that could spread like wildfire through the hearts of the world. And 238 pages of the most funky looking holiness book design you can shake a stick at will fill in the blanks.